RESTORING NEW TESTAMENT CHRISTIANITY

Featuring: Alexander Campbell, Thomas Campbell, Barton W. Stone, and Hall L. Calhoun

D1470432

DR. ADRON DORAN

ISBN# 0-89098-161-2

DEDICATION

To my beloved, Mignon, who has walked by my side for sixty-six years and has stood with me in endurance, encouragement, and consolation.

No one could ask more of a dedicated helpmate than she has been.

CONTENTS

FOREWORD

Dr. Adron Doran is a man for all seasons. He is a man among men, standing head and shoulders in every way above multitudes of peers.

The Man and the Moment is the title of an excellent little book, written in 1927 by John Allen Hudson, a friend of mine. The book is a study in the life of Alexander Campbell. Hudson observed, "The circumstance—and the man must be united before one can come to be numbered with the immortals."

Hudson quoted from J.J. Haley in *Debates That Made History*, "when the man and the moment come together, as they always do when a great providential task is to be achieved, something happens." Hudson applied this principle to the man, Alexander Campbell, and the moment, Campbell's time in human history, for a great providential movement.

This principle can be applied appropriately to Dr. Adron Doran, and his time in human history in Kentucky. The State of Kentucky, and environs, are certainly different and better because Dr. Doran has lived there. He has served effectively in many capacities, and his service is first class in everything he has done or does. He is a scholarly Christian gentleman of the first order. He is, as John Allen Hudson would say, "a man of parts."

Dr. Doran has been highly respected as a faithful, Biblical, gospel preacher for sixty-eight years. He served as President of Morehead State University for over twenty years, and is President Emeritus of Morehead State. He is a first class gospel preacher, a first class scholar, and a first class Restoration historian, all qualities of which are a very valuable asset to the man and to the Lord's church.

Dr. Doran has participated in scores of educational leadership service positions, and Christian councils and organizations, from his appointment by President Lyndon B. Johnson to the National Advisory Council on Education, to his role as President of the Kentucky Education Association, to his help in founding International Bible College, to his position on the board of directors of Freed-Hardeman University.

Now, there is the man! He was able to crowd in his busy schedule vital presentations at Crieve Hall church of Christ in Nashville,

Tennessee, and Nashville School of Preaching and Biblical Studies, September 22-26, 1996.

Sunday morning he spoke twice on "The New Testament Church," in a strictly Biblical, scholarly, masterful way, glorifying the church for which Christ died, and urging people to find forgiveness, safety, and salvation therein. Sunday night he spoke on "The Restoration Movement," delineating the necessity of such a movement and how it came about. Wednesday night he spoke of "Difficulties Encountered With the Restoration Plea."

At the Nashville School of Preaching and Biblical Studies, Dr. Doran spoke Monday evening on "Barton Warren Stone and Cane Ridge," Tuesday night on "Alexander Campbell and Brush Run," and Thursday evening on "The Christian Scholar—Biography of Hall L. Calhoun." In all of these presentations, Dr. Doran demonstrated himself as a scholar eminently qualified, and as an effective communicator of the gospel message as well as a first class Restoration historian.

We believe the man and the moment have come together in a significant way in Dr. Adron Doran. Those who heard the presentations at Crieve Hall church of Christ and Nashville School of Preaching and Biblical Studies came away with a clearer view of the New Testament church and where we are in human history. His coming made a tremendous difference for good to the glory of God.

The series was well attended. All presentations were recorded and are available in cassette tapes, audio/visual tapes, and in book form. We thank God for this availability, and pray the materials will be widely used. We commend highly their use, and believe they will make a great difference for the good of the church and to the glory of God, wherever used and sincerely studied.

Paul M. Tucker, Minister
Crieve Hall Church of Christ
Nashville, Tennessee
June 12, 1997

PREFACE

This volume is a transcription of six lectures delivered at the Crieve Hall church of Christ and the Nashville School of Preaching and Biblical Studies during the period of September 22-26, 1996 on the theme of restoring New Testament Christianity.

The series of lectures was arranged by Paul Tucker with the complete endorsement and full support of the Crieve Hall eldership and Dan Winkler, the minister. We trust that this overview of the Restoration Movement, as meager as it is, will provide a greater insight into the struggles and a deeper appreciation of the events and persons of the early 1800's.

We hope we presented something to those who heard the lectures and to those who read them that will call us all back to the Biblical principles advocated by the early restorers and defended by loyal gospel preachers and dedicated elders today.

The task of transcribing the lectures from the taped spoken word to the written word has proven to be a most difficult chore. We are indebted to Winston Moore, with 21st Century Christian, who heard the lectures and accepted the task of publishing them as a "labor of love," his most excellent staff, his efficient secretary, Maxine Brown, who typed the document, and Dr. Sue Berry, Professor Emeritus of English at David Lipscomb University, who spent hours of her valuable time in editing the manuscript.

My personal good wishes and deep gratitude are expressed to all of those who have lent words of encouragement to me in the study of the Restoration Movement since my retirement from the presidency of the Morehead (Kentucky) State University twenty years ago. The more intense my research, the greater has been my regard for those who extended themselves to restore New Testament Christianity, the ancient order of things, the gospel of Jesus Christ, and the Church of Christ. My appreciation reaches out to those of the present century who are raising their voices to call men back to the Bible.

Adron Doran

Chapter One
The New Testament Church

A vital, and yet too often neglected, topic in this age is the Restoration Movement. It is worth every possible effort to establish a basis, not only for interest in the Restoration Movement, but also for further study and research on that great American movement which had its culmination in the soil of our own nation.

Unfortunately, there are many individuals and some entire congregations of the church of Christ showing little or no interest in the Restoration Movement. In fact, there are some who have become openly antagonistic toward a discussion of the movement. They want neither part nor parcel in any effort to understand its nature and implications. Other individuals are totally indifferent. They have no interest whatsoever in learning anything about it. They are not against it, but they are not for it; they are coldly indifferent toward any discussion of the subject.

Reasons for these existing attitudes toward the Restoration Movement vary. Some people are uninformed, while others are grossly misinformed. There are writings on the subject which clearly reveal that certain would-be scholars do not possess accurate information about this great movement; consequently there is no way for them to cultivate and communicate a correct perspective.

But regardless of unsatisfactory treatments, the Restoration Movement has been, and still is, focused on calling individuals back to the Bible. Therefore, it is absolutely essential that there be first of all a thorough understanding of what the Bible teaches. We *must* be clear on those things that should be restored. So a study of the subject of the Restoration begins with a close and open-minded study of Bible teaching about the New Testament church, which early restorers were seeking to bring back into being. That was one of their prime objectives. They were dedicated not only to going back to the Bible, but also to identifying the nature and practices of the New Testament church in order that they could pool all resources to restore that institution which one can read about in the Bible. It is obvious that there must be an understanding of what the church is before successful efforts can be made toward restoring it to its pristine state. Once a student of the Bible learns what the church was in the first century, then he is at a point where he can comprehend what it should be today. The pattern must simply be brought back into focus.

It is important to note, in the beginning of this study, that the church is *not* a product of society. Society did not produce the church. When we talk today about modifying the purpose of the church in order to meet current social needs, we either have a faulty understanding of what the church is, or we do not know how properly to meet social needs. It is not the prerogative of society to dictate to the church, for it is not a product or property of society. Now, in contrast, we see that political entities, educational institutions, and industrial systems are products of society, *but the church is not!*

Furthermore, the church is not a denomination, so it cannot be measured by denominational standards or by sectarian ideals. Some in the church of Christ today apparently consider themselves enlightened when they speak of the church as "an old, tired, worn-out denomination." Well, it is not! The church is not tired. It is not worn out. *And it is not a denomination!* So it is inappropriate and wrong to discuss the church in denominational and sectarian terms or to identify it as a denomination functioning alongside various other religious institutions which are in existence.

Finally, and just as emphatically, the church is not a product of the Restoration Movement. The Restoration Movement did not produce the church. The Restoration Movement proposed to bring back into existence the church of the Bible, with every revealed trait restored and identified.

The church of Jesus Christ as described in the New Testament was a dominant concern of those associated with the Restoration Movement. It should be as well the dearest preoccupation of Christians today. After all, Jesus Christ and the church were in the eternal purpose of God. The church was no accident, no whim, and no happenstance. It was not an afterthought. It was in the eternal purpose of God. Jesus Christ Himself, as the Word of God, became flesh and dwelt among men. God purposed to send Jesus Christ. He further purposed that this same Jesus would build the church.

The plan for Christ and His church was in place from the beginning. The familiar words of Genesis 3:15 which were revealed to Satan and recorded by Moses as the conversation with God about the coming Jesus Christ and the establishing of the church:

And I will put enmity between thee and the woman, and between thy seed and her seed; it shall bruise thy head, and thou shalt bruise his heel.

The important part of this annunciation was that God purposed that Jesus would come and close the gap of separation between man and God, reconciling man once more to God. The church served that same purpose (Ephesians 2:16).

In Ephesians 3:7-12, the apostle Paul wrote to the church at Ephesus affirming that he had been made a minister "according to the gift of the grace of God." How came God to appear to him? How was it that he was led to obey the gospel of Jesus Christ? Paul said that he had been called to obedience and to become a minister "according to the gift...of God." He saw and accepted God's intention and purpose for his life. God appeared to Paul that he might "preach among the Gentiles the unsearchable riches of Christ." That was the reason. God did not appear on the road leading to Damascus in order to convert him. Ananias accomplished that feat when he taught him the Word of the Lord more perfectly and baptized him to wash away his sins. Paul understood his mission and God's intent: God appeared unto me, said the apostle "that I might preach the gospel, I might open the eyes of the Gentiles, and I might preach to them the unsearchable riches of Christ." Paul was "to make all men see what is the fellowship of the mystery." Where had this mystery been concealed? Paul said that it had "from the beginning of the world been hid in God." Not until this time had God chosen to reveal it, and now Paul was to go about as a minister preaching the unsearchable riches, revealing the gospel and making the mystery known. So the purpose of God in sending Jesus Christ and in calling the apostle Paul and others to be ministers of the Word, was to make known the gospel, the unsearchable riches of Christ, the mystery of God which had been hidden from the foundation of the world.

Straightway, Paul shifted attention from his own responsibility to that of the church. His function had been carried out. Now it was the responsibility of the church to make known "the manifold wisdom of God." In effect, Paul declared that he had done what God purposed for him to do. He said that he would stand "before the judgment bar of God" to give an account of the fulfillment of his calling. Now the responsibility must shift from him to the church: it was God's purpose and intention for the church "to make known the manifold wisdom of God according to the eternal purpose which he purposed in Jesus Christ our Lord" (Ephesians 3:7-12).

So what is the purpose of the church? Why, it is to uncover the great mystery of God which had been concealed until the apostles were given the responsibility for preaching it. Now it becomes the obligation of the church today to do that same thing, just as God intended from the beginning.

If the church does not make known the unsearchable riches of Christ today, who will? What institution will take it upon itself to play that role? Well, someone might suggest that the Democrats can do it. No, the Republican Party will do it. Or the Reform Party will accept the responsibility. Well, God never intended that the church would be of this world; neither should anyone expect a worldly party to preach the gospel.

Some may say: let the gospel be taught in the public schools. No, God never intended that either. Admittedly, this country has gone astray in denying individuals to have contact with Christianity and the Bible in public schools. But God never did intend for public education to make known the unsearchable riches of Jesus Christ. So the question continues to echo: if the church does not do it, who will? No institution, except the church, has been founded and designed to make known the mystery of the gospel of Jesus Christ. A second question must follow: if the church does not do that for which it was created, then what is its purpose, its reason for being? There is no known purpose or justification for the existence of the church if it rejects its responsibility and ignores its obligation to preach the gospel of Jesus Christ. So the Bible says that God purposed that Jesus Christ would come. He purposed that the church would make known the unsearchable riches of God through Jesus Christ our Lord.

Now the church entrusted with the stewardship of these unsearchable riches was not called to our attention yesterday, the day before yesterday, or last month. The church was made known through ancient prophecy, and wisdom demands that we conscientiously familiarize ourselves with Christ's church in prophecy.

The first clear example presents the classic case of old Nebuchadnezzar and Daniel the prophet. Under this infamous ruler of Babylon, Israel had been subjected to cruel slavery and captivity. When King Nebuchadnezzar experienced a bothersome dream, whose substance eluded him, he sought help in recalling the dream and in interpreting its meaning. At last, Daniel was given the formidable responsibility. Being a prophet of God, Daniel was equal to the challenge. He explained to the king that the dream meant that the Babylonian empire over which he presided represented a civil government to be followed in order by the Medo-Persian kingdom, the Greek kingdom, and eventually the Roman kingdom. Daniel explained to Nebuchadnezzar that the elements of his dream represented these kingdoms. "But," the prophet added that "in the days of the Roman kings, the God of heaven would set up a kingdom which shall never be destroyed; it would stand forever." Daniel was not merely talking about civil kingdoms; he was also referring to the kingdom of God. And this kingdom would be set up by God in the days of the Roman Empire (Daniel chapter 2).

Daniel was not the only man of God used in revealing the church through prophecy. Isaiah declared that the house of God would be established in Jerusalem: "for out of Zion shall go forth the law, and the word of the Lord from Jerusalem (Isaiah 2:3). Now God is going to Jerusalem to set up His kingdom. And the Word of the Lord and the law of Jesus Christ would come from Zion. How did these prophets know this? The Holy Spirit revealed to them what was going to happen, and on the basis of their faith in the revelations, they prophesied.

Prophecies continued into the New Testament. Matthew says, "In those days came John the Baptist preaching in the wilderness of Judea and saying, 'Repent ye, for the kingdom of Heaven is at hand'" (Matthew 3:1-2).

Daniel had said centuries before that God would set up a kingdom. Isaiah had said that it would be established in Jerusalem. Now, John the Baptist was preaching in the wilderness of Judea, that the kingdom was "at hand." The time was near. It was approaching. It was imminent, immediate! Jesus Christ Himself said "that the law and the prophets were until John. Since that time the kingdom of God is preached and every man presseth into it" (Luke 16:16). Jesus is saying that there would be an end to the law of Moses! There is to be a fulfillment of the prophecies of God. The law of Moses is to be abolished. The kingdom of God will be preached, and men will become citizens of that long-anticipated kingdom.

The church was in prophecy. It is important to see the church in the teachings of the prophets as the purpose of God is being revealed.

A second phase of the study of the church is also of critical importance. That phase concerns the church in promise. One does not have to go to the prophets alone to find promises of the establishment of the church. Jesus called His disciples to Him (Matthew 16:13ff) and inquired of them, "Whom do men say that I am?" After they had shared with Him street talk and marketplace speculations, He asked a heart-searching question: "Whom do ye say that I am?" To Simon Peter's response, "Thou art the Christ, the son of the living God," Jesus said:

> Blessed art thou, Simon Barjona: for flesh and blood hath not revealed this unto thee, but my Father who is in Heaven. And I say unto thee, that thou art Peter, and upon this rock I will build my church; and the gates of Hell shall not prevail against it.

More is derived from this announcement of Jesus than the futurity and the determination of His promise. There is the awareness of that thread that runs true in the promise of God even into the very teachings of Jesus Himself. He said, "I will build." The promise was to be accomplished in the future, but the declaration was sure and clear: "I will build it; I am determined to build it. Even though the gates of hell should swing ajar and I enter into the hadean world and all the powers of Satan pounce upon me, I will build my church."

Then Jesus turned to His disciples and made a startling addition to His announcement:

> There be some of them that stand here, which shall not taste of death, until they see the Kingdom of God come with power. (Mark 9:4)

The apostles must have looked at each other in astonished anticipation. "Get ready," He was telling them. Get ready, for you will still be living to see the kingdom come and experience the power with which the kingdom has been promised to you.

Luke, in giving a part of the Great Commission, quotes Jesus as saying:

> And, behold, I will send the promise of my Father upon you: but tarry ye in the city of Jerusalem until ye be endued with power from on high (Luke 24:49).

No doubt the apostles believed what Jesus said. They made themselves subject to His orders. He had clearly directed them to prepare for the kingdom's coming, to go to Jerusalem where they would wait to be endued with power from on high. They were responsive to His promises. Spurred by faith, loyalty, and anticipation, they set out for Jerusalem.

When the apostles asked Jesus whether He would restore the political kingdom to its original place in Jerusalem, He replied:

> But ye shall receive power, after the Holy Spirit is come upon you: and ye shall be my witnesses both in Jerusalem and all Judea and in Samaria and unto the uttermost parts of the earth (Acts 1:8).

"Wait for the power," the apostles were told. God had promised them power, and they came to Jerusalem to receive it. They were to leave Jerusalem as Jesus' witnesses.

Would you see the purpose that God had in sending Jesus Christ to establish the church? Would you see the prophecies of Daniel and Isaiah and others regarding the coming of the kingdom of the Lord? Would you see the promises of Jesus Christ when He said, "I will build my church?" Well, if you see them, you cannot escape the conclusion that the purpose was manifested, that the prophecies were fulfilled, and that the promises of Jesus Christ became a reality on the day of Pentecost in the city of Jerusalem in the year A.D. 33 (Acts chapter 2).

The apostles were in the city with all the rest of the disciples, who had gathered together, to await the fulfillment of the Lord's promise. And it was there on that day that the Holy Spirit came, as Luke described the event. The house in which they sat was filled with the sound of "a mighty rushing wind and cloven tongues as if fire sat upon each of them." The apostles "began to speak in other tongues as the Holy Spirit gave them utterance" and devout Jews "from every nation under heaven" heard the apostles speak, each one in his own language (Acts 2:2-6). The promise of "power from on high" had been kept.

But the people questioned the purpose of what was taking place. Finally Simon Peter said unto them, "this is that which was prophesied. This represents the purpose of God. This is the fulfillment of the promise of Christ that has now come to pass. The gospel as the mystery and the unsearchable riches of Jesus Christ is being declared."

Simon Peter preached the first gospel sermon under the authority of Christ on that day of Pentecost. Peter's message pricked the listeners' hearts, moving them to cry and ask "what shall we do?" The answer from Peter rang out loud and clear:

> Repent and be baptized, every one of you, in the name of Jesus Christ for the remission of your sins, and ye shall receive the gift of the Holy Spirit (Acts 2:38).

From that historic day of Pentecost, the church is no longer seen in purpose, no longer written about in prophecy, no longer offered in promise. It is now perceivable in reality. On that day those who accepted the Word were baptized and there were added to the church three thousand souls (Acts 2:41). And from that time on those who were being saved, or should be saved, were added daily to the church (Acts 2:47).

Now this assembly in Jerusalem constituted the universal church. It also constituted a local congregation of the *universal church*—the only *local congregation* in the world, since the apostles had not yet gone out to witness in other parts of the earth. The church was established here, and its identity was that of a universal body and at the same time identifies as a local congregation of saints. The congregation was autonomous in all of its practices.

Next we look from the church in Jerusalem to other cities and villages throughout Judea, Samaria, Galilee, and the uttermost parts of the earth. The apostles became busy establishing local congregations, each one of them a part of the universal church which Jesus had purchased with His own blood.

The church in Jerusalem constituted three thousand souls on the day of Pentecost when the first believers were baptized. The Bible goes on to say that, at a later time, there were as many as five thousand members. Then the Bible depicts the church as becoming a multitude—a *multitude* of people! There are some impressively large congregations today, but would any one of them be said to constitute a multitude? How large was that multitude of people who had believed and been baptized for the remission of their sins? Then the Bible reports that the church was being multiplied. The multitude multiplied! Finally, it is said that the multitude multiplied greatly. How many obedient believers were there in Jerusalem making up the church of our Lord and Savior Jesus Christ? No one knows! Some speculate that there must have been at least a hundred thousand members of the church in Jerusalem. That is not certain. What is certain is that this congregation in Jerusalem was visible as the obvious and clear fulfillment of the purpose, prophecy, and promise of God. In addition, other local congregations of the church were established, with each one forming itself into a local body of obedient believers. One can be confident that all of those people who were baptized on the day of Pentecost returned to their homes in remote corners of the earth and busied themselves with preaching the gospel and baptizing believers. How many local congregations were thus established by them is, of course, unknown. But one can read about the nationalities of those present in Jerusalem on that day and see a multitude pouring out of Jerusalem in all directions which must have resulted in a multiplicity of congregations throughout the world.

A little later, further impetus was given to the spread of the gospel from Jerusalem. Luke reports, in Acts chapter 8, that a great persecution arose against the church in Jerusalem, and members were scattered abroad. As they dispersed, they went everywhere preaching the Word and, as an effect, establishing local congregations of the church. Everywhere these disciples, who were scattered abroad, went, they preached the gospel and established and organized local congregations.

An example of one going into all of the world is Philip, the evangelist, who traveled into Samaria. The Bible says that he preached Christ. He preached the Word of the Lord. He preached the things concerning the kingdom of God. He told all who would listen about the church and about how the church had been established in the city of Jerusalem. He told about the three thousand who had obeyed the gospel and about how God had added those baptized believers to the church. Luke says that when Philip preached the gospel, the Samaritans were obedient. Men and women were baptized. The result was the establishment of congregations of the church in Samaria. Congregations just like the one in Jerusalem. Philip did not go there and establish groups of individuals separate and apart from the one in Jerusalem. Each congregation was exactly like all of the others, following the exact same pattern in work and worship.

The apostles in Jerusalem, hearing news of Philip's preaching to these Samaritans things concerning the Kingdom of God and of the baptisms which ensued, decided to send Peter and John to Samaria to investigate the situation. They were made glad when they observed that the grace of God had appeared and been made known to the Samaritans, who had availed themselves of its power.

On the return trip to Jerusalem, according to Luke's account, the company preached the gospel in many villages of the Samaritans. Prior to their visit, churches had been established in Samaria to which they preached the gospel and they established other churches in Samaria. That is precisely the way the gospel of Christ spread, and that is the way the church of the Lord became a prominent institution in all of Asia and Europe. Surely no one would doubt that the Ethiopian eunuch, whom Philip baptized on the road leading from Jerusalem to Gaza, returned home to share his new found faith about Christ, about the gospel, and about the kingdom. Along with his duties as Secretary of the Treasury to Queen Candace, he likely requested and received permission to share the good news far and wide. It is improbable to believe otherwise. He may have baptized numerous believers in the land in which he lived. It is not too far-fetched to conjecture that he may even have taught and baptized Queen Candace. In that case, what a powerful influence would then have been exerted in the cause of multiplying saved souls and establishing congregations!

By now the point should be clear. When one begins to study about the church of Jesus Christ, he starts in the city of Jerusalem on the day of Pentecost in 33 A.D. Then he watches the kingdom spread and spread. And this increase—this spreading—was the result of the preaching of the gospel. The taking of the gospel to the far corners of the earth and the acceptance of it and obedience to it, brought about the formation of congregations of obedient believers who came together in worship and went forth to serve God Almighty.

Well, the apostles left Jerusalem and traveled everywhere preaching the Word. Their journeys can be traced! As they wended their way through different regions in the Lord's cause, new congregations sprang up. Luke reports in Acts 9:31 that the churches in Judea and Galilee and Samaria were at peace. They were at peace and the peace they enjoyed emanated from a unity based on total acceptance of the Bible as the rule of faith and practice. The disciples all achieved and maintained peace on the same order. Luke explained that they were "walking in the fear of the Lord," and they were all experiencing that same identical "fear of the Lord." Further, Luke said, they were all "walking in the comfort of the Holy Spirit." The Holy Spirit was with them, and He brought comfort to them. Luke says they were "edified" and then he adds that they were "multiplied." This same thing was happening all over the land. The church was being established. The church was being organized. Individuals were worshiping God in spirit and in truth as citizens of the kingdom. In Acts 14:21-23, Paul's journey is traced from Antioch to Lystra and Derbe and Iconium. What was Paul doing in this area? Well, he was preaching the gospel. But what was he doing as he preached? Luke said that he "confirmed the souls of the disciples." So there were already disciples in these towns. Paul had not made all of them, but he confirmed those that he found. He must have assured them by telling them that they heard the truth. They had obeyed the gospel. They were worshiping God in spirit and in truth. And thus he confirmed these disciples. Luke goes on to say that Paul "exhorted the brethren to continue in the faith," that faith "once for all delivered unto the saints." He no doubt urged them not to depart from that faith. Furthermore, he "commended them to the Lord on whom they had believed." They had believed in Jesus Christ. They had obeyed the gospel of Jesus Christ. They had submitted their lives to Jesus Christ. Paul commended the disciples, and then warned them about the tribulations in the kingdom. Now if they were not in the kingdom, would Paul have bothered to warn them against the tribulations to be suffered in the kingdom? He was not warning outsiders. He was warning the members of these churches about the tribulations to be anticipated and endured in the kingdom.

Luke said that Paul also "ordained elders in every city and in every church." Here is presented the organization of local congregations. Here, clear and plain to observe, is the perfection of the Lord's plan. Paul demonstrated the pattern in each of these congregations. The apostle later wrote to the church in Thessalonica and said that it became "followers of the churches in Judea which were in Christ Jesus" (1 Thessalonians 2:14). Think of it! There wasn't an iota of difference between the Jerusalem congregation and any other congregation in any locality throughout the land. They were alike, all of them! These congregations followed the example of the churches in Judea because the churches in Judea were in Christ Jesus; therefore, these congregations were also in Christ Jesus our Lord. All of the congregations followed the exact same organizational pattern, without the slightest deviation. They took the pattern set by the church in Jerusalem, and followed that organizational pattern down to the smallest detail. Nobody gave any thought to an organizational pattern for the *universal* church. They all thought in terms of ordaining elders in every local congregation, not a universal set of officers. That idea emerged later, during the time of the apostasy of the church. Titus was left in Crete to ordain elders there (Titus 1:5). Paul called elders of the church in Ephesus to meet him at Miletus, where he delivered his vale-dictory speech to them (Acts 20:22). Wherever Paul went, congrega-tions were established on the same organizational pattern.

Every congregation was also identical to every other church in their pattern of work and worship. *There were no exceptions.* None of them embroidered upon or veered from the plan that God had authorized—the plan that was first actuated in Jerusalem. Luke says that the church, or the disciples, in Troas met on the first day of the week to break bread. Paul met with them and preached to them (Acts 20:7). So, here was a congregation in Troas meeting on the first day of the week to break bread. Then one finds the church in Corinth doing the same thing (1 Corinthians 11). Paul taught the Corinthian saints in correct-ing the mistakes they were making with regard to observing the Lord's Supper. He did not tell them that partaking of the supper was optional or that they might choose to observe it on Saturday night or on Tuesday night. Instead, he corrected the manner in which they were doing it, assuring them that he had received these instructions from the Lord. The Lord instructed Paul about the organization of the church and also about acceptable worship. Worshipers not only observed the Lord's Supper, but also gave of their money on the first day of the week. They were commanded to lay by in store as the Lord had prospered them (1 Corinthians 16). Paul admonished the church in Ephesus and with the church at Colosse it set the pattern for singing psalms and hymns and spiritual songs, making the melody in their hearts (Ephesians 5:19). Scriptural worship in all congregations fol-lowed the same pattern.

Finally, it must be understood that all individuals throughout the land who constituted the church of Jesus Christ our Lord were admit-ted under the same plan and on the same conditions. *All converts* recorded in the New Testament did exactly the same thing to become members of the church of our Lord. Every individual believed, repent-ed, confessed faith in Jesus Christ, and was baptized in water for the remission of sins, and then God added the individual to the church. How wonderful it would be today if there were this same regard for the church among the people that the apostles held. Oh, that it were possible to say by one and all that "by one spirit we were all baptized into one body" (1 Corinthians 12:13).

CHAPTER TWO

THE RESTORATION MOVEMENT

Unfortunately, we cannot bask in the past glory of the establishment of the church and the spread of the gospel. The breath-taking accomplishments by the apostles and nameless other Christians who lived and died during the first century to make the church a reality represent only the beginning of the story. It is necessary to move to the sad task of examining the process by which the church of the New Testament apostatized and forsook the old paths. Eventually, a great Reformation Movement took place in Europe. The effort to reform the apostate church attested to the fact that the distance between practices of existing religious institutions and the church of Christ which was established in Jerusalem was difficult to measure. Still, the Bible pattern was not sought by the reformer and used to ward off man-made changes and innovations. At last, the old world moved around to the time when men made a strong concerted effort which brought about what is referred to in history as the Restoration Movement. Before that, though, the establishment of the church, the great apostasy, and the Reformation Movement all took up about 1800 years of human history. These significant events and far-reaching implications merit far more extensive consideration than they are usually given today.

The Church of Jesus Christ was established in the city of Jerusalem on the day of Pentecost in A.D. 33, in accomplishment of the purpose of God, in fulfillment to the prophecies of the Old Testament, and in accord with the promise of Jesus Christ our Lord. Local congregations were established throughout Asia and Europe until all individuals had an opportunity to hear the gospel and to come to an understanding of the church.

Even during the first century though, the apostles saw a drifting away from the New Testament order of things and recognized signs of apostasy as congregations and individuals began to depart from the faith. Much of the writing of the apostles was directed to the brethren as warnings, in the hope that apostasy would be averted. The apostle Paul called the elders of the Ephesian church to meet him at Miletus, where he delivered to them his moving valedictory address (Acts 20:28-32). Whether he ever visited with them again is not revealed. But he said to the elders on that occasion, "After my departing shall grievous wolves enter in among you, not sparing the flock." Those scavengers whom Paul likened to vicious preying animals were even then lying in wait for the time when the apostle had gone. They would move into the church and devour the flock as grievous wolves would bring havoc upon the sheepfold of the shepherds. Paul told the elders, "Of your own selves, (from among the eldership), shall men arise, speaking perverse things to draw away disciples after them." Now, that was a sad commentary and an ominous prophecy! It was an admonition to the elders of the church in Ephesus to watch, not only for their own souls, but for the precious souls of those over whom the Holy Spirit had made them overseers.

The apostle Paul later wrote to the church of God in Corinth and said to the members of that congregation in that ancient city; "I fear lest by any means as the serpent beguiled Eve through his subtlety, so your minds should be corrupted from the simplicity that is in Christ." Now, the church in Corinth must have thought that it was sailing along in fine fashion. The members considered themselves to be doing exceptionally well, but Paul said to them "be careful about your encounters with the devil." Satan seduced Eve through his subtleness, and corrupted her. Paul feared that by those same means which Satan used on Adam and Eve, he would seduce the Corinthian brethren and lure them away from the simplicity that is in Christ (2 Corinthians 11:1-3).

The apostle Peter engaged himself in giving the same kind of warning. He wrote to those whom he said had obtained like precious faith through the righteousness of God and admonished these righteous people of precious faith; above all else to beware lest they be led away by the wicked one and fall from their own righteousness and steadfastness.

In this same manner, the apostles continued earnestly to warn the church of the danger of apostasy and being led away. The apostle Paul seems to have concluded the whole matter when he wrote to the young evangelist Timothy and said: "The Spirit speaketh expressly that in the latter times some shall depart from the faith, giving heed to seducing spirits and doctrines of demons." These apostates will act as if their consciences had been seared by a hot iron, speaking lies as hypocrites. This is an established fact, Paul solemnly assured them; and they must heed the warning or be lost. Laying a serious charge upon Timothy, he continued, "...put the brethren in remembrance of these things, (and if you do), then you shall prove to be a good minister of Jesus Christ" (1 Timothy 4:1-6).

A troubling question today is this: are members of the church pleased to hear preachers "put us in remembrance" of the possibility of apostasy? In many cases we decide that one who approaches the subject must be something of an extremist or a fanatic. How tiresome to be addressed about the dangers of drifting away! Besides, a growing tolerance for deviations from the Bible pattern in the name of individual differences and individual freedom and love for the brethren makes the subject of apostasy a hazy superstition, a bogey man without the power to frighten. But, all the same, there still exists real dangers of departing from the faith. Every day we are confronted by error. We are faced with threats to our own steadfastness. Some twentieth century Christians think the bearer of warnings is meddling instead of preaching, but Paul said Timothy would be a good minister of Jesus Christ if he warned the church against these ever present dangers.

Sadly, in spite of all the warnings by the apostles and their clarion calls to defense against errors, the church began a slow and gradual process that led it into a state of apostasy. This was a condition in which the church appeared to have lost every semblance of identity with the New Testament. Where was the New Testament church? Did not the prophets declare that it would last forever? Yes, indeed. Only God can say where it was during the dark ages. Some individuals have speculated that it went underground, that there were many faithful individuals during the great apostasy who still believed the truth and practiced it while hiding themselves from the powers that would have snuffed out their lives. That well could have been the case, for during the Reformation Movement there emerged groups which had continued to believe and obey the truth. It is said, and likely true, that there is only one generation between faith and apostasy. Our next generation should be taught the dangers of apostasy, the perilous dangers of drifting away and departing from the faith.

Let us turn now to a brief look at the historical records which touch upon what happened to lead the New Testament church into apostasy. The first step taken toward apostasy was in the field of organization. In the beginning, of course, the local congregation exercised complete autonomy. The local congregation had elders, deacons, evangelists, and teachers exactly as the Bible required (Philippians 1:1). Such is the only organization that the New Testament authorizes. But at an early point in time, men began to change the pattern in an attempt to organize the church on a universal basis. They lost sight of the autonomy of the local congregation and began to reorganize the church, thereby corrupting the whole system of Christianity. This man-shaped institution came to be known as the Roman Catholic Church. The apostate body then created the Papacy, and all people were made subject to the Pope, who reigned from Rome. A universal organization was the first step, a giant one indeed!

The second step into apostasy was in the area of doctrine. Once the New Testament organizational pattern had been discarded, it was not difficult to move on to tamper with sound doctrine. About 325 A.D. a great controversy arose among the bishops of the church. The controversy was led by Arius, a bishop of the church in Alexandria. Confusion resulted from the bishops' inability to agree on the relationship among God, Christ, and the Holy Spirit. Constantine, the Roman Emperor, saw that a division within Christendom, at that time, would be detrimental to his civil empire. So he endeavored to bolster his sagging realm by calling 318 of the bishops to meet him at Nicaea in the province of Bithynia for the purpose of talking matters over and arriving at a consensus. Constantine presided over the momentous assembly. After a period of heated controversy, the bishops finally wrote and adopted what is called the Nicene Creed. Regardless of what the Bible taught about the relationship among Christ, God, and the Holy Spirit, they wrote down in a creed what the *church* was supposed to believe, what the *church* was to advocate, and what doctrine would be promulgatged as the teachings of the *church*. As time passed, ecclesiastical councils were called to meet in various places and each group added to the creed its concept of church doctrine and practice. Some of the doctrines which were added were the doctrine of indulgences, the doctrine of purgatory, the doctrine of auricular confession, and the doctrine of infant baptism. The councils also gave the church the authority to prescribe "ordinances." How simple it was, once the first step was taken and the Nicene Creed was written, to amend the creed and write subsequent additions to it which would virtually cover the entire waterfront. Soon what could be likened to a simple, unadorned garment had been so covered over by bows, ruffles, lace, and all manner of adornment that not one thread of the original garment could be detected.

The third step in the great apostasy took place in the area of worship. When the church leaders perverted their organizational pattern and changed the doctrine to which they had been committed, then of course they also changed the pattern required of assemblies gathered to worship the Lord. One of the first changes in worship had to do with the observance of the Lord's Supper. The Bible is as clear on the subject of taking the Lord's Supper, the Communion, the breaking of bread, as it could possibly be on any subject. But the apostate congregations so perverted the worship of the Lord that the Supper became a Latin Mass or what was called the "Eucharist." They so completely perverted and corrupted the observance of the Lord's Supper that the concept of transubstantiation was introduced. They taught that the bread became the literal body of Jesus Christ. They resorted to a practice in which they would not let the members handle the bread because it was too precious to be touched. Members would march up before the priest, who would lay wafers on their tongues. Officials also taught that the fruit of the vine became the literal blood of Jesus Christ. They would not pass the fruit of the vine around, lest some worshiper might inadvertently spill the very precious blood of Jesus Christ in handling the cup. Instead, the priest would drink the juice of the fruit of the vine himself for the rest of the audience in observance of the Supper. That is the perversion of the Lord's Supper which became a practice in the apostate church, a practice about which one may freely read on the pages of secular history. They later corrupted the *a cappella* music of the church, when devotees met together and lifted their voices in singing praises to God, making the melody in their hearts. The New Testament Church sang psalms and hymns and spiritual songs, but the apostates added mechanical instruments of music to the singing. The corruption of the worship of our Lord altered the whole Biblical concept of public worship. The Bible ordained plan was obscured, scrapped and discarded!

Such were the conditions that prevailed by 1215 A.D. during the time of King John's reign in England. Remember that King John wrote the great Magna Carta, a document designed to give civil liberty to the English people. Well, that document granted religious freedom too. So delegates of the church met in Rome for the Fourth Lateran Council and repudiated King John and announced that the church was supreme and that the Pope had all power and all authority in heaven and upon earth. The council further decreed that the Pope had never sinned, that he was incapable of sin, that he would never sin. The Pope was indeed declared to be infallible and that he could speak *excathedra.*

When the Pope spoke, he did not speak necessarily according to the Bible, but "in addition" to it. He could speak over and above and beyond what the Word of the Lord said, and what the Pope spoke had the same impact and the same binding power upon the church as the Bible itself. Now, that is a sad state of affairs. But we must recognize that the church of our Lord had apostatized and become an entirely different organization from the one set forth in such clear terms in the Bible. The church had so perverted its organization, its doctrine, and its worship that it was not recognizable as the Biblically presented and ordained church.

What happened at that point in time to break the stranglehold which the Catholic Church had on the people? The Pope was the sole authority in civil and ecclesiastical affairs. He put his stamp of approval upon every civil act of the emperors in the nations under the domain of the Catholic church. There are two or three landmark events which began to undermine papal power. One of them was what historians call the "papal schism" or division among the popes of the Catholic church. They were greatly at odds with one another, with all of them striving for power and authority and each of them claiming to be the successor to the apostle Simon Peter. They claimed that upon Simon Peter, Jesus Christ had built the church, instead of the confession of Simon Peter that Jesus is the Christ, the Son of the living God. This schism within the papacy resulted in one Pope reigning in Italy, another in France, and another in Turkey. At one time, three popes were reigning at the same time, and every last one of them claimed to be the successor to Simon Peter. Well, obviously, two of them had to be wrong! Actually, all three of them were wrong. None was a successor to Simon Peter, and none should have claimed the authority that was bestowed upon the papacy by the Catholic church. In fact the apostle Peter was not a pope of the New Testament Church. It is not surprising that this schismatic situation had a great effect upon loosening the stranglehold upon the communicants.

A second force which served to weaken the pervasive power of the Catholic church was the Italian Renaissance. Intimidating as the word may seem, it simply signifies a "revival of learning and a restoration of nationalism." At this time France, England, Germany, Switzerland, and many other nations were under the domination of a foreign Pope. He sat in Rome and from there ruled the world. Finally, citizens began to rebel against the sovereignty of a foreign Pope, and this movement gave rise to nationalism, marked by a desire to bring about a state-church relationship within their own countries. Scotsmen desired to organize the Church of Scotland. The English wanted to create the Church of England. So it was that nationalism began to prevail and to erode the stranglehold of the Papacy.

Furthermore, the Renaissance Movement was characterized by a revival of interest in learning. During the medieval period, there had been a loss of interest in learning—coupled with practically non-existent opportunities. But in the thirteenth century there was a renewal of interest in studying the Hebrew and Greek languages. With renewed interest in these two ancient languages, individuals developed the ability to read the Old Testament and the New Testament in the original languages. The Bible had been handed down to the people in Latin. The old Vulgate which Jerome had translated from the Greek and Hebrew into Latin was all they had to read and besides, the Bible was almost literally chained to the pulpit. Now scholars were translating the Bible into the languages of Hebrew, Greek, English, and German, so that the common people could at last study the Bible for themselves. Another phenomenon contributing to the spread of learning was the invention of the printing press. The Guttenberg press, which made possible the printing and circulation of religious literature and the Bible, opened the door for all to read the Bible in their own languages. Opportunity had arrived like a fresh breath of air and again the papal stranglehold was weakened.

A third movement which tended to undermine the supremacy of the Catholic church was the Protestant Reformation in Europe. Groups of individuals had become weary, worn, and burdened with the organizational pattern, with the false doctrine, and with the corrupt worship of the apostate church. They set out to reform these corrupt practices and to correct the false teachings of the Catholic church. This is the essence of the Protestant Reformation. It did not cross the leaders' minds, seemingly, that they ought to take the Bible and seek out the Bible pattern and restore that pattern. The reformers thought instead of accepting the pattern of the church as it was and trying to reform that pattern. Thus began a period of reformation in which Martin Luther in Germany, John Calvin in Geneva and France, Ulrich Zwingli in Switzerland, and Henry VIII in England made attacks upon the domination by the apostate church. Now Henry VIII, in the role of reformer, was quite different from the others. He had previously been considered by the Pope to be a "defender of the faith." He was so designated and complimented for his ability to defend the faith against the other reformers and the leaders of the Renaissance. The king had become tired of living with Catherine of Aragon as his wife. He wanted to put her away and take for his wife Ann Boleyn, a maid in waiting and an attendant to the queen. The Archbishop of Canterbury refused to present his request for a divorce from Catherine to the Pope in Rome. Finally Henry dismissed the Archbishop and appointed another who would present his case to the Pope. When the Pope denied a writ of divorcement to Henry VIII, the monarch called the English Parliament into session and asked this body to authorize a separation from the Catholic church in Rome. He himself would become head of the Church of England. Thus was established what has come to be known as the Anglican or Episcopal church. Yes, Henry VIII was a reformer of a different ilk! Luther, Calvin, Zwingli, and others decided that what they ought to do was to take the Bible and prove to the established order that it needed to reform itself. Familiar to most are the details of Martin Luther's 95 Theses which he wrote and nailed to the door of the Wittenburg Church. History records that the Pope excommunicated Luther and pronounced an interdict upon Germany because that country refused to banish Luther and his teachings. These were critical times through which individuals went in searching for the truth and the way.

One must hear with disappointment and disillusionment that an overview of the Reformation Movement shows that it actually did little more than create a system of denominationalism and sectarianism in the religious world. There were no religious denominations before this time. Christianity was under the control of the Catholic church, but as a result of the proposed reforms, there emerged a variety of sects and a potpourri of denominations which fashioned themselves according to the names and teachings of individual reformers. The Puritans and the Pilgrims brought this confused state of affairs to

America. Soon these religious leaders became as dogmatic as the Catholic church had ever been in the old world, with respect to the beliefs and practices which they bound on the people with little room for tolerance.

In the midst of this situation characterized by division, confusion, confrontation, and controversy, the concept of the Restoration Movement emerged and began to take form. Its champions immediately faced hard questions. What could they do that the reformation had failed to accomplish? What must be done about rampant denominationalism? How can a healing be brought about in a land where Christendom is severed into so many groups and unity is only a fond memory? Well, in response to these challenging questions, the concept of the Restoration Movement was born. Instead of talking about reforming the *status quo*, instead of talking about reforming the corrupt practices and the false doctrines of the apostate church, concerned religionists discarded the tainted body, threw it all overboard, and dived into the Bible to find out what the New Testament taught and dictated as practices. They sought to find in the Bible what constituted the organization of the church and what it did in worship. Barton Stone took the Cane Ridge Church back to Jerusalem instead of leaving it in Rome. Alexander Campbell took the Brush Run Church back to Jerusalem. They bypassed all of the arrangements of the denominations of that day. They said, "We'll go back to Jerusalem for the original!"

What was the Restoration Movement? What is involved in the process of restoring the New Testament church? For that matter, what is the process for restoring anything? Well, the dictionary offers a simple definition such as this: "To restore is to return to an original state after loss of essential character." A restorer goes back to the original, to the first pattern. The church had lost its original state. It had lost its identity. It had lost its status as the body of Christ. Barton Stone, Alexander Campbell and others went back to the original to restore the body of Christ that had lost its essential character. That is what they decided must be done.

Where on earth did they come upon that concept? They got it from the Bible, where there are to be found many examples of restoration. David, in penning the twenty-third Psalm, said, "The Lord is my Shepherd, I shall not want." And among other blessings which the Lord had bestowed upon him, David said that God had *restored* his soul. Surely no one needed his soul restored more than David did. In Psalms, chapter 51, he confessed that his sin of adultery was ever before him. He cried out for a restoration of his soul. He needed to return his soul to its original state, for it had lost the essential quality of righteousness, godliness, and purity. David knew what he was talking about when he used the word restore. In the sixth verse of the first chapter of Acts, the disciples asked Jesus, before He left the earth and ascended on high, "Will thou restore again, at this time, the kingdom to Israel?" Did they not know what they were talking about? Well, of course they did. They knew exactly what they thought was about to happen. They expected Jesus Christ to bring back into existence the old Jewish system, the Law of Moses and the rites and rituals of Judaism. Now they eagerly inquired, "Will you restore that?" The disciples asked about that kind of restoration and wondered if Jesus Christ would bring it about at that time. In Galatians 6:1, Paul said that if any man has been overtaken in a fault, those who are spiritual should restore such a one. What would they do to the man who had been found in sin? They would take him back to the state he was in before he was overtaken in a fault. They *restored* his soul. They restored his spiritual life. Thus they brought him back to the original state from which he had fallen. Why, even old Zacchaeus (Luke 19:8) knew what he was talking about when he used the word restore. Remember how he ran ahead of Jesus and climbed up into a sycamore tree because he was too short to see over the heads of the crowd? He could look down from the tree and observe Jesus as He passed that way. Jesus said to him, "Zacchaeus, come down out of that tree: salvation has come to your house." Zacchaeus, a tax collector for the Roman government, said he would give one half of all that he had to the poor; and if he had defrauded anybody, taken unjustly from anybody, that which was not his just deserts, then he would restore fourfold. He would give the money back. He would put the money back just as it was before he stole it.

All of these individuals knew exactly what restoration meant. If there is still doubt regarding the way individuals dealt with the subject during Bible times, go far back to the days of Amos and Nehemiah. There is an account of the Jews' coming out of captivity and returning to Jerusalem to restore the temple. They discovered the law of Moses and read it to the people as it was in the original form. They set about rebuilding the walls of the City of Jerusalem which had fallen down and repairing the gates which had been burned. That is one of the greatest restoration projects to be found anywhere in the Bible. It qualifies as a restoration project. The concept is clearly exemplified in this account, for these Jews were restoring the original.

Well, that is exactly what the restoration leaders were talking about doing in the early 1800's. Now the seed of the Restoration Movement had been planted earlier, in far-off Scotland. The movement was led by those who had separated from the Church of Scotland, which had accepted the Presbyterian system of government in that nation. The separation was led by John Glass and his son-in-law, Robert Sandeman. They were assisted by Grevill Ewing and the Haldane brothers. In Glasgow and Edinburgh during the late 1700's, they proposed to abolish the system by which the church and state had been united and, once that relationship had been removed, to return to the Bible, accepting it as their only rule of faith and practice. What was the effect? They gave up infant baptism, they met on the first day of the week and broke bread as disciples had done during the New Testament period, they preached the gospel of Jesus Christ as it was set forth in the Bible, and they taught believers to obey the gospel of our Lord by being buried with him in baptism. The work of Glass, Sandeman and the Haldanes was the beginning of the Restoration Movement in Europe.

Restoration in America developed in what is known as the Southern Movement in Virginia and North Carolina. In those states, a man by the name of James O'Kelly, along with Rice Haggard and Clement Nance, were advocating the concept of a Restoration Movement. Nance and Haggard later went to Cane Ridge in Bourbon County, Kentucky during the time that the Last Will and Testament of the Springfield Presbytery was being written. At last, in our own country, the trek back to the first century had begun!

From across the ocean other seeds of religious change had blown. The followers of John and Charles Wesley not only affected the intellectual and spiritual climate of England, but also in America. A number of Wesley's followers met in the city of Baltimore, Maryland, where they organized what they called the Methodist Episcopal Church on Christmas Day in 1784. In addition to adopting a name for their society, they ordained Francis Asbury as the Bishop and named James O'Kelly as superintendent of a district in North Carolina and Virginia. Societies had been formed in England by the Wesley brothers. It may be surprising to learn that John Wesley never left the Episcopal Church. When he died, he was buried in the ecclesiastical garb and robe which he had worn as a priest in the Anglican church.

When the members of Wesleys' societies came to America, they did not have shepherds. They did not have ministers to tend their flock. Wesley tried to get the Episcopal priests, who were already in

America, to act as shepherds, but they refused to do so. When the Revolutionary War came on, most of the Episcopal priests, who were Whigs, high-tailed it back to England as soon as the shooting started. The whole Episcopal system in America was left without priests. Under these circumstances, Charles and John Wesley decided they must do something for their followers, so they called delegates to meet with Asbury in Baltimore, Maryland at the Christmas conference. The second meeting of this conference was held in Manchester, Virginia, on November 28, 1792. At this meeting James O'Kelly and Rice Haggard raised their objections to the system which had been established as the Methoodist Episcopal Church. They withdrew from the meeting, resigned from the conference, and decided to call themselves Republican Methodists. This country was, after all, a new nation, a new Republic, independent and frisky-minded. O'Kelly and Haggard considered themselves religiously independent, so they took the name of Republican Methodist to emphasize the independence they were bent on claiming.

A general meeting of these seceders was called on August 4, 1794, to meet at the old Lebanon meeting house in Surrey County, Virginia. What were they going to do now? They were out of the Methodist Church. They were no longer affiliated with the denominations in any way. They had objected to the authority granted to Bishop Asbury, and they wanted nothing more to do with the Episcopal system of government. They knew what they were *not* going to do, but what *should* they do? That was the question. They talked for a while during the Lebanon meeting about the situation, and finally Mr. Hafferty arose and said, "I move that we take the Bible as our only rule of faith and practice." Now that was a significant departure from the discipline of the Methodist Episcopal Church. This seceder was declaring, "We should have nothing to do with human confessions of faith." A unanimous vote reflected the group's readiness to go along with Mr. Hafferty's radical proposal, as their opponents saw it. Rice Haggard then stood up with a Bible in his hand and said, "If we're going to take the Bible as our only rule of faith and practice, I read in Acts 11:26 that the disciples were called 'Christians'! He proposed to drop the name Republican Methodist and call themselves Christians and Christians only. Haggard suggested that they take to themselves the name Christian only, now and forever more. Isn't that fascinating? Does not that move you when you observe the peace, quiet and tranquility of the restored Church of Christ and find that you can worship God in spirit and in truth as a member of the body and as a citizen of the kingdom? Here in Virginia were men striving and struggling diligently to determine what to do with denominationalism as it existed at that time. The words which were uttered on that day were revolutionary and insightful, and came from the hearts of brave men.

Another group was to be found in the New England states which had no knowledge of what was transpiring in North Carolina and Virginia. The New England Restoration Movement was led by Elias Smith and Dr. Abner Jones, both of whom were young Baptist preachers. They had become dissatisfied with what the Baptists taught in the Philadelphia Confession of Faith and they were looking in their search for the truth. They accepted the idea of taking the Bible and the Bible alone as the basis for what they would preach and practice. As a result, they established independent churches of Christ throughout the New England states, particularly in New Hampshire and Vermont. They called the individuals Christians and the corporate bodies churches of Christ. Smith published what he called the *Herald of Gospel Liberty*, reputed to be the first religious journal to be printed in America. In this journal Smith and Jones set forth their objectives.

Another effort was being made as the Western movement. It was not connected with the Southern Movement at all. The leaders knew nothing about Rice Haggard, James O'Kelly, or Clement Nance. However, they later made their acquaintance. Haggard went to Kentucky and taught B.W. Stone to adopt the name Christian. They knew nothing about Smith and Jones up in New England. The Western Movement began in Kentucky, Tennessee, and Southern Ohio, led by Barton Warren Stone and in Pennsylvania, Northeastern Ohio, and northern Virginia, led by Thomas Campbell and his son, Alexander.

A troublesome question to Stone and the Campbells was how to go about perfecting the movement. It is one thing to talk about restoration in theory and quite another thing to put it into practice.

The process of restoring New Testament Christianity was a long and gradual process. It took a long time for the church to apostatize, and it would take a long time to bring it back to its original state. What were Stone and the Campbells endeavoring to do?

In the first place, they proposed to restore New Testament Christianity. Christianity as it was known in the 1800's was not New Testament Christianity. It did not have New Testament teaching as its base. It was so perverted and corrupted that it was unrecognizable as the system that one reads about in the Bible. Certainly it had lost its identity with what the writer James described as "pure religion and undefiled before God and the Father." So Christianity must be restored and attain the traits attributed to it in the New Testament.

Secondly, leaders thought in terms of restoring the ancient order of things. They believed that there was a Biblical order of things. They believed there was an ancient order of things as Campbell described it. They believed that there was a Biblical pattern. They believed that God created the earth and the heaven according to a pattern. They learned that Moses built the Tabernacle according to a pattern which God showed to him, and they further believed that Noah built the ark according to a blueprint. They decided that there was a pattern for the ancient order of Christianity and they must return to it. They concluded that if they preached the same gospel that Simon Peter preached on the day of Pentecost and hearers believed and obeyed that gospel, they would be saved and God would add them to the church.

The third thing they agreed to restore was the gospel of Jesus Christ. They asked themselves how New Testament Christianity could be restored, how the ancient order of things could be restored unless the gospel of Jesus Christ was restored? The necessity of restoring the gospel was first indicated by Walter Scott. Scott had come from Scotland to Pittsburgh in 1819 and was converted by a Haldane preacher, George Forester, who baptized him in the Monongahela River. Scott preached all over the Western Reserve in Northeastern Ohio and pretty well clarified what is meant by the gospel wherever he spoke. As Scott and others looked around, they found the same situation existed that Jesus observed while He was upon the earth. Matthew reports in chapter 15, verses 8 and 9, what Jesus said about what He saw:

> This people draweth nigh unto me with their mouth and with their lips honor me, but their hearts are far from me. In vain do they worship me, teaching for doctrine the commandments of men.

That is also what the restorers found among the worshipers of their day. Walter Scott wrote a volume in 1836 setting forth the gospel which he had been preaching since 1827. The book was titled *The Gospel Restored*, and was the first record by any restorer claiming that there are certain facts, commands, and promises of the gospel. He said the facts are that Jesus died, was buried, and raised from the grave. There are certain commands of the gospel Scott pointed out which are binding upon all that we must believe, repent, and be baptized. And, furthermore, he identified certain promises given in the gospel which are the remission of sins, the gift of the Holy Spirit, and eternal life. All of those elements constitute the gospel, and Scott urged the restoration of that gospel. Scott introduced what has been called the "fingered exercise." He would teach school children the names of his fingers by pointing out one is faith, one is repentance, one is baptism, one is remission of sins, and one is the gift of the Holy Spirit. Children learned these as the names of their own fingers. Then they would go home and tell their parents what they had learned and that a man who had taught them words preached at the school that night. Soon crowds filled every schoolhouse where Walter Scott preached.

Finally, men in different areas of the country set their hands and their hearts to restore the New Testament church. Restore New Testament Christianity? Yes. Re-establish the ancient order of things? Of course. By all means! Return to the gospel of Jesus Christ? Certainly! But when all of these things have been done, what will be the result? Why, you will have also restored the church of the New Testament. You will have the church of the Lord and Savior Jesus Christ in existence which He purchased with His own precious blood and built upon the foundation of Christ the Son of the Living God. What procedure did the restorer follow?

In the first place, they proposed that all man-made creeds and confessions of faith be abolished and abandoned. They must go about the task of abolishing their creeds as if they were clearing new ground to plant a crop. If you don't know first-hand that clearing new ground is a dreadfully hard task, just believe me. Every human creed must be uprooted, pulled up by the roots and moved away completely. The Lutherans had adopted the Augsburg Confession of Faith. The Presbyterians had adopted the Westminster Confession of Faith. The Baptists had adopted the Philadelphia Confession of Faith. The Episcopalians had written the English Prayer Book, and the Methodists had reduced the 39 articles of the English Prayer Book to 24 and adopted the smaller document as their Discipline. But all of these man-made documents had to be abolished and abandoned and replaced by the Bible and the Bible only.

Then what? That one Book, the Bible, must be accepted as the only rule of faith and practice.

Thomas Campbell, in 1807, at the home of Abraham Alters, said, "We will speak where the Scriptures speak, and we will remain silent where the Scriptures are silent." Others have added along the way that "we will call Bible things by Bible names, and we will do Bible things in Bible ways." And "in matters of faith, unity, but in all things, love. The restorers proposed that if we abolish creeds and confessions of faith, and take the Bible as our only rule of faith and practice, then we should unite with all believers under the individual name Christian and the body of Christians under the corporate name Church of Christ. That was a simple proposal yet complex, compound, disturbing, and confusing to people who were holding tenaciously to their traditions and systems.

We have recited in brief what is the Restoration Movement. In retrospect we ponder what if these courageous, loyal, dedicated, and devoted men had not labored tirelessly to bring us out of denominationalism and into the church of our Lord? What if they had not taught what they did, when the outcome seemed, at times, in question? Had Stone and the Campbells not accomplished what they did, we know not what the situation would be like today. We have accepted the teaching of Stone and Campbell wherein they taught the word of God. One thing is certain; it would be a pitiable situation indeed if these men, and hordes of unnamed supporters, had not given themselves to the leadership of this great movement. Thank God for their lives and their efforts! Let us attach the same significance to the Bible and to the church as they did. God rest their weary souls.

CHAPTER THREE
DIFFICULTIES ENCOUNTERED WITH THE RESTORATION PLEA

The Restoration plea is just as simple as the Bible itself. No proposition could be clearer. The dedicated apostle Paul called the way of the Lord "the simplicity in Jesus Christ." But simplicity did not assure swiftness and ease where the Restoration Movement was concerned. Yet no organized effort that men have attempted since the first century has meant more to the world than the Restoration of New Testament Christianity, the restoration of the church of our Lord and Savior Jesus Christ, and in bringing the gospel once again into proper focus. That is the plea. It is one thing to declare oneself a champion of the plea, and stack arms with opponents who deny the validity of that plea and quite another matter altogether to throw oneself into the task of implementing that plea. It is the difference between theory and practice. Remember that the leaders of the Restoration Movement had declared themselves free of all creeds and confessions of faith. They had decided to accept the Bible as the only rule of faith and practice. But when it came to putting these decisions into effect, it became another matter. What difficulties were hovering and lurking out here waiting to be confronted when any effort was made to put the plea into effect? Obviously, there would be pitfalls along the way. These intelligent leaders would not have expected the course to be smooth and uneventful. Indeed, the road was rocky, and there were many ups and downs. There were high mountain peaks, but there were low, dark valleys too. Great challenges faced all who were dedicated to the cause.

One of the things that presented great difficulties again and again was the opposition of the denominational and sectarian communities into which the restorer entered. They were stating their plea and asking the religious denominations and sects to abandon their human creeds and confessions of faith and take the Bible alone, which meant that most denominations would be eradicated; they would be put out of business. It is no surprise that proponents of the Restoration Plea incurred wrath at least, and aroused what sectarians considered to be righteous indignation. There was bitterness and plenty of it. In many cases, the leaders of denominations in the targeted communities expressed outright hatred. The adherents to the plea were called New Lights, Stoneites, and Campbellites. Such an atmosphere of animosity makes a sad chapter in the history of this plea. Some of the scars still remain.

Beyond the opposition of the sectarian leaders, the preachers of the restoration message were troubled with the dissension that entered the rank and file of the Restoration Movement. Nothing today hurts the church or cripples the cause of Christ more than dissension within the ranks. It clips the wings of the message and lames the feet of the messenger. It is easier and less discouraging sometimes to deal with confrontations with denominational preachers than to handle disturbances within the church by those who have defected from the truth. Such troublemakers are difficult to deal with. Today the church is dealing with some seceders from the faith just as it did in the first century and in the early days of the Restoration Movement.

Within a short time after the signing of the Last Will and Testament of the Springfield Presbytery, four of the six notable signatories had defected: Richard McNemar, John Dunlavy, Robert Marshall, and John Thompson. A few years (1811) after the movement began, Marshall and Thompson returned to the Presbyterian Church. Richard McNemar and John Dunlavy defected to the Shakers. The Shakers, founded by a woman (Lee) who claimed to be the female counterpart of Jesus, sent representatives into Southern Ohio and Kentucky. They first appealed to Barton Stone, but to no avail. By and by, they had succeeded in persuading McNemar and Dunlavy to leave Stone and the Restoration Movement and take up the Shaker cause. The choice of these two men is a sad commentary on human judgment and decision. Both of them died rejected and poverty-stricken, completely separated from everything they had started out to accomplish. Yet this kind of defection, disappointing as it is, should not be too shocking or even surprising. The apostle Peter wrote about such inconstancy during Bible times. He wrote of a sow that, after having been washed and made clean, she returned to wallowing in the mire (2 Peter 2:29). And he told of the dog which had returned to his own vomit. Peter was talking about the same kind of behavior which was exemplified by McNemar and Dunlavy. He is talking about people like Marshall and Thompson, who severed connections with Presbyterianism only to turn back to it. Both turned their backs upon the cause they had espoused and went back to the denomination in which they had originally held ordination. They returned to the Westminster Confession of Faith simply because Barton Stone and David Purviance would not agree to write a creed that was less latitudinarian than the Bible itself. Only two of the original group now were left: Barton Warren Stone and David Purviance. Naturally, the departure from the cause they pled, by close and trusted colleagues, depressed the two remaining men; but more importantly, it hindered the success of the movement and mitigated against its immediate spread. Stone said this was one of the darkest hours of his life. He wilted under the burning awareness that he had been deserted. He was fearful for his own life.

The same thing that happened to the associates of Stone was happening in the camp of Alexander Campbell. Sidney Rigdon, a brother-in-law of Adamson Bentley, was one of the outstanding Baptist preachers in the northeast quadrant of Ohio—the Western Reserve. Bentley and Rigdon came to visit with Campbell at his home in Bethany. They spent an afternoon, a night, and a day with him, talking about the plea that Campbell advocated. They agreed with Campbell's position in all respects. After Campbell had shown Rigdon where he was wrong, he said, "If I have preached one error, I have preached a thousand errors in my time!" Rigdon joined the Campbell movement, wholly and without reserve. When the time came (1823) for Campbell to go to Washington in Mason County, Kentucky, to conduct a debate with W.L. McCalla, a Presbyterian preacher, Rigdon saddled up his horse and rode two hundred miles with Campbell from Bethany, Virginia over to Washington, Kentucky to serve as the chief note taker of the debate. He took copious notes, from which came the publication of the debate. He was seemingly committed to the plea. Later Rigdon came in contact with Joseph Smith, who at that time had found some tables of stone on which he claimed the Mormon Bible was written. Rigdon promptly joined Smith and became one of the powerful influences in founding what they chose to call the Church of Jesus Christ of the Latter Day Saints, now referred to as Mormons. Convincing proof exists that if Rigdon had not defected and gone to join with Smith, the Mormon movement would not have made it off the ground. It would have died without much notice and been dismissed as the fitful and fanciful imagining of a deranged man.

Though Campbell suffered a great loss when Rigdon forsook the movement, he was soon to be consoled by his association with Jeremiah Vardeman, one of the best known Baptist preachers in Kentucky. This man was big from two standpoints: he was famous and his name was a household word among Baptists in Kentucky, and he weighed 350 pounds, thus measuring big in avoirdupois as well as in reputation. When Campbell arrived in Washington, ready to debate McCalla, he selected Vardeman to be his moderator. They spent a great amount of time together during the debate. Following the end of the debate, Vardeman invited Campbell to go to the Old David's Fork Baptist Church east of Lexington and preach to his congregation. Right speedily there developed a strong, warm relationship between them. There was a time when Campbell would have almost expected himself to desert the cause rather than Vardeman. But desert he did! When Vardeman defected from the Restoration Movement and returned to the Baptist Church, Campbell sadly responded: "If I had been in Kentucky at the time, I would have been able to persuade Vardeman not to leave us." Wishful speculation, that! The fact is, he did leave the movement and renounced all that he had stood for and moved to Missouri. He not only defected, but he became an active antagonist of the movement. He confronted every preacher of the Restoration Movement who went to Missouri. Jacob Creath, Jr., moved to Missouri from Kentucky and became one of the greatest objects of Vardeman's ridicule. This kind of bitterness and bickering hindered the cause and hindered it greatly. These were indeed difficult times! Stone and Campbell were having difficulty deepening their roots in the soil of the Restoration Movement. There are brethren today who are still suffering under this same difficulty as they strive to extol the plea in all its simplicity. Many have also defected from the church in these latter times, and others will likely follow. Both Christian schools and churches may follow after them in defecting from this great effort. *That is our fear.*

The second difficulty to be noted involves the problems that Stone, Campbell, and their associates encountered as they applied the principles of the plea to the actual practices required of them to put the plea into effect. Now, they had all grown up in denominationalism, and suddenly, without opportunity to watch anybody else do what they were proposing to do, they recognized that their plea was completely contrary to all of the concepts and practices in the denominations in which they had held membership. They were being forced to remove themselves from sectarian affiliations and from creeds and disciplines if they applied the plea. Well, that was traumatic. That was difficult. It was disturbing to them. They were faced with an inevitable decision to leave what they had previously taught if they were to implement the plea in faith and practice. It would take time to achieve this goal. The difficulty of making the plea and practice the same is demonstrated at the Cane Ridge Church and at the Brush Run Church. These people had great faith in what they were doing. After all, they were not fly-by-night people. They were not individuals who had suddenly appeared on the religious scene. They were individuals who had become deeply embedded in the religious concepts and practices in which they had been reared. Some of Barton Stone's trouble came because of his speculation regarding the relations among Christ, God, and the Holy Spirit. He simply had difficulty in dealing with what he called the "Trinity" and in deciding how to relate God and Christ to each other and how to relate the Holy Spirit to God and Christ. So intense had his speculation become that Campbell considered Stone to be an Arian, meaning that Stone had accepted the doctrine of Arias, a bishop in the church at Alexandria who was responsible for the Emperor Constantine calling 318 bishops in the year 325 A.D. to settle this problem of the "Trinity" which was troubling the early churches. Campbell said Stone had gone back to Arian beliefs. Stone later announced that he had renounced all of his speculative holdings.

When the Campbells were baptized in Buffalo Creek by Matthew Luce, together they spoke for seven hours. In his speech, Thomas

Campbell said to the crowd, "I am astonished. I am astounded at what we are doing. I had preached Presbyterian doctrine for thirty-five years, and when I announced that we would "speak where the Scriptures speak and remain silent where the Scriptures are silent," and when I wrote the Declaration and Address in 1807, I never thought I would be brought to this point." He never dreamed he would be in the Buffalo Creek with Matthew Luce, a Baptist preacher, baptizing him, along with his son, his wife, and his daughter upon a confession of their faith in Christ. He just could not conceive that this would happen when his great plea was actually applied to the practices of himself and others.

Aylette Raines is a classic example of an individual diligently striving to bring practice into line with plea. Raines was a "restorationist" preacher, not in the sense used in connection with the Restoration Movement. Rather, he was called a restorationist because he believed that at some time God would gather all the people who had ever lived or were still living together, and he would save them, every one. God would restore salvation to everybody, no matter how they had lived, no matter what the state of their souls were at the moment of death. God would eventually grant salvation to everyone. In essence, this was a doctrine of universal salvation which Raines preached all over Kentucky and Ohio. While preaching in Ohio, he went to hear Walter Scott, who was conducting revivals on the Western Reserve. By and by, Scott converted Raines. He later attended an annual meeting of the old Mahoning Baptist Association along with Thomas and Alexander Campbell. Raines applied for admission as a preacher to the Association. Many members and leaders objected strenuously. "Why," they exclaimed, "he holds to the 'restorationist' beliefs and we do not want him among us." Raines assured them that he had renounced that doctrine except that he still held to some of it as a matter of opinion. The delegates to the Association did not think that was good enough. And so Thomas Campbell stood before the assembly and chided them for their attack on Raines. Campbell told them that he himself still held to parts of Calvinism as matters of opinion. "I have not been able to totally divorce myself from Calvinism yet," he said. "I still believe in some of the Calvinistic tenets, but I hold them as opinion only. So let us accept Raines as a member of our fellowship because he too holds his concept of restorationism as opinion."

This instance clearly exemplifies the difficulties these men had in separating faith from opinion. Thomas Campbell was admitting that he still held some of the doctrine of Calvin as a matter of opinion.

Campbell defended Raines in holding some parts of "restorationism" as opinion.

Just listen to those words of Thomas Campbell. Think of the sentiments he was expressing! How on earth could Campbell hold an opinion that was contrary to the Word of God? Opinion can be held but it must be in harmony with the Word of God, and it is the responsibility of the Christian to see that it is. An opinion which does not harmonize with the Word of God has no place in one's mind and heart. An opinion regarding religion must not be held contrary to the Word of God.

The early church also had difficulty in separating itself from the practices of the Law of Moses. Of course, the early Christians had trouble giving up Judaism in all of its tenets. They had trouble with eating meat given as animal sacrifices, fornication, the burning of incense, circumcision, and coming to entirely accept Christianity. Their background as Jews and Greeks gave them something constantly to reconcile or to give up. The early Christians finally worked themselves through all of the difficulties and came to believe in Jesus Christ as the Son of God, to accept the church which He purchased with His own blood, and worship God in spirit and in truth. It was the same kind of challenge which those in the Restoration Movement had to face in leaving denominationalism.

It was especially difficult for the early restorers to harmonize their former beliefs and practices with the Bible teaching on baptism. Many, strangely, have always had a "hang-up" about baptism. It has been a red flag before the eyes of many people. They are incited to all kinds of emotions when baptism is the topic of preaching. The mode and the design of baptism are usually topics of heated discussion. How are people baptized? Why does one submit to the act of baptism? Clear, simple words are not enough to remove the swaddling clothes of mystery and misunderstanding on the part of some.

Early Christian restorers who were advocating the restoration plea could hardly take what they had believed from childhood and apply it to the New Testament practice of immersing for the remission of sins. In all fairness, it should be remembered that, in their earlier days, all of them had been sprinkled; not a one of them had been immersed. Barton Stone, as an infant in Tobacco, Maryland, had been sprinkled by an Episcopal priest, Thomas Thorton. Thomas Campbell, no doubt, had sprinkled all of his children while they were yet in Ireland. Every last one of them had been sprinkled before coming to America, for that was all they knew, so that is what they practiced. The question of infant baptism and sprinkling as a form of baptism was raised in the

Stone movement first by Robert Marshall who advocated immersion. He was the first among his peers to announce that he no longer believed in the practice of sprinkling, for he was convinced that only immersion was Biblical. John Thompson was a strong aspersionist. He believed, taught, and practiced sprinkling. Stone was so greatly concerned that he feared Marshall might leave the movement and join the Baptists, since the Baptists were the only ones on the frontier who were practicing immersion. So great was the disturbance over baptism that some of the people at the old Bethel Church in Fayette County, Kentucky, where Marshall preached, wanted him to sprinkle them instead of immersing them. He refused to do so, and they proceeded to send for Stone to come from Cane Ridge over to Bethel to sprinkle them. The contention became so great among them that finally a conference was called for the purpose of discussing the mode and design of baptism. The meeting was held at Cane Ridge, and those in attendance, after long hours of hard study, agreed to disagree. They finally decided to let the immersionist immerse and allow the aspersionist to sprinkle; those who were immersed would not despise those who had been sprinkled, and those who were sprinkled would not despise the immersed. Easier said than lived out, day by day! But having come to this decision, they broke camp and went their ways. It is hard to imagine such a meeting and such an outcome.

In 1807, a young woman who was a member of the Cane Ridge Church went to Barton Stone and asked him to immerse her. People had been admitted as members of the Cane Ridge Church without any act of obedience except that they believed Jesus Christ to be the Son of God, and they affirmed that God had forgiven their sins. Stone made arrangements for the woman's baptizing in old Stoner Creek, on the north outskirts of the city of Paris, Kentucky, and a large crowd of people gathered on the banks of the creek to watch Stone baptize her. Among those in the crowd were Reuben Dooley and David Purviance. Now she was the first person among the Stone group to be immersed, so everyone was particularly eager to witness the act. As preparations were being made, Purviance asked Stone to allow him and Dooley to make speeches. Well, that was a good place to make a speech. I have listened to many speeches at baptizings. They took the opportunity to make very long speeches. Perhaps they came to Stoner Creek with their minds made up as to what they wanted to do. Or maybe their minds were at work during the lengthy sermons, leading them to amazing decisions. However, it came about, the two men ended up by asking to be baptized. So Stone first baptized the woman and turned around to hear David Purviance ask him to baptize him. When Dooley heard Purviance's request of Stone that he immerse him, Dooley asked Purviance to "put him under the water." So Dooley and Purviance were both baptized on this most eventful day. Writing about this incident later, Purviance said that Stone himself had not been baptized at the time, nor was he baptized that day by either Purviance or Dooley. Stone baptized the woman and the two men, yet he himself had never been immersed! However, Stone wrote later that he and all of the preachers baptized one another and then turned around and immersed the members of their congregations. They concluded that if they were authorized to preach the gospel, they also had the authority to baptize believers.

When Thomas Campbell announced his motto that he would "speak where the Scriptures speak and remain silent where the Scriptures are silent," the people immediately began to ask what the implications of the statement were with respect to infant baptism. How would Campbell's motto affect age-old cherished beliefs and practices regarding sprinkling infants for baptism? Well, Thomas Campbell said that the baptism of infants was merely inferential. He claimed that one must infer that the Bible teaches infant baptism. What a sly escape mechanism that was! Infer infant baptism, no indeed! Alexander Campbell did not believe what his father said and he answered his father by saying, "If we do what you have announced, then baptism of infants and sprinkling for baptisms are out." Alexander had to face this same argument later when he debated W.L. McCalla in 1823. This well-known Presbyterian preacher contended that infant baptism was comparable to circumcision. The Jews circumcised, and the Christians baptized. McCalla said babies were circumcised under the law of Moses and now infants should be baptized. "Well," asked Alexander Campbell to McCalla, "What are you going to do with the little girls? The Jews did not circumcise little girls, so little girls do not enter this comparison which you make for little boys." McCalla also said that infant baptism is inferred from the case of Lydia of Thyatira, whom Paul encountered at a riverside prayer meeting in Philippi and baptized. Campbell responded that to get infant baptism in the case of Lydia, it must be inferred that her household was composed of infants. When Paul baptized the household of Lydia, he would have had to baptize infants. If the inference is made that babies were baptized as a part of the household of Lydia, one must also infer that Lydia was married. Nobody today knows whether she was married or not. If she had been married, her husband may have died, or she may have left him at home because he was a poor salesman and she could make better deals selling the purple cloth herself. One must further infer that if she were married she had children, but not all married couples do. Too, one must infer that if Lydia had children some of them were infants. By inference, which is not necessary, there is authority for infant baptism. Cat tracks in ashes which the wind blew away! (Acts 16:11-15).

Well, McCalla was stumped by Campbell's arguments. He could not prove by the Bible that there were children in Lydia's household. His argument went down the drain.

When Alexander Campbell was refuting McCalla's argument, he was at the same time refuting his own father's argument that infant baptism is merely inferential. When Alexander Campbell read the proof sheets of the Declaration and Address which Thomas had delivered in 1807, Alexander said to him that he must abandon and give up infant baptism and other practices if indeed they were going to do what Thomas said they were going to do. The son said to his father, "You have said that we cannot accept anything in the Scriptures except what is an expressed concept or an approved example." Now Alexander fully believed in the principle which Thomas had expressed. But he said to Thomas regarding the Declaration and Address, "You are telling it just as it is. But if we follow your interpretation of the Bible, then we will have to give up infant baptism."

Most members of the church today have followed the same interpretation of the Bible which the Campbells enunciated (1 Peter 4:11). We have been taught to learn the direct commands of the Bible. We were taught to identify approved apostolic examples and to find certain statements from which to infer the truth and accept direct commands of Jesus Christ. But some brethren have emerged today with different ideas. They say we need a new exegesis. We need to change our way of interpreting the Bible. We cannot follow the old method in these modern times. However, these liberal brethren have never made it quite clear what that new method is and what the results would be.

The third area of difficulty for the restorers arose from what name they should call themselves. Why bother with the name to be called? What's in a name? A great deal! And in this instance, much pain and anguish were experienced. With their avowed intention of returning to the Bible and being guided by it, we might think that the matter of nomenclature would be an easy one to settle, but it was not easy. Barton Warren Stone wanted to remain a Presbyterian. He wanted to organize a new Presbytery and make it a part of the Kentucky Synod.

He wanted to continue the same relationship with the Synod that had existed under the Transylvania Presbytery. However, the Synod would have nothing to do with such an arrangement. But when Stone and his associates saw the light of the good news, they understood that it was not possible to longer wear the name "Presbyterian." They were going to have to let go of their old relationship. This idea was brought to their attention by Rice Haggard, who came to Cane Ridge from North Carolina. Haggard taught Stone and his associates that they ought to call themselves Christians and Christians only just as he had taught those associated with the James O'Kelly "Christian Connexion." So Stone accepted the name "Christian." Immediately there arose the question, "What will we call the corporate body?" Well, if they were going to honor Christ by wearing His name as individuals, they should wear the name of Christ to indicate that they belong to Him as a body. Thus, Stone and his associates adopted the name "Christian" for individuals and the name "Church of Christ" for the corporate body. The Brush Run Church was called the Church of Christ. The Cane Ridge Church was called the Church of Christ, and these names are engraved on the tombstones of Alexander Campbell and Barton Stone. The tombstone of Barton Stone erected in the church cemetery in 1847, says that it was placed there by the Cane Ridge Church of Christ. William Rogers wrote a letter to Mrs. Stone after Barton's death and signed it as an elder of the Church of Christ at Cane Ridge. Stone himself wrote a letter to the Cane Ridge congregation in 1843, a year before he died and addressed it to the Cane Ridge Church of Christ. Now when somebody wants to take the name Disciples of Christ back to Cane Ridge, he had better go back to Jerusalem first and start all over again. The Disciples in their effort to rewrite Restoration History cannot take their movement of latter days back to Cane Ridge or Brush Run and use the same name they are wearing today without doing violence to the Restoration Movement itself. It is true that Alexander Campbell wanted to call the restorers Disciples and ended up causing a racket over the name. Men like John T. Johnson, John Rogers, Walter Scott, Raccoon John Smith, John Allen Gano, Aylette Raines, and Barton Stone all wanted to call themselves Christians. But Campbell said they ought to be called Disciples because the word disciple is more ancient than the word Christian. Campbell claimed that the followers of Christ were called disciples before they were called Christians. However, it was with a lower case "d" and not an upper case. He also said that the name disciple is more descriptive. In truth, though, the name disciple is not more descriptive than the name

Christian. Christian means that the wearer of the name belongs to Christ. Disciple merely means a learner of Christ. Campbell went on to allege that the name disciple was unappropriated by any other religious group. He was offended with the "Christian Connexion" which James O'Kelly and his group had organized in Virginia. They called themselves Christians, and Campbell simply was not willing to copy the name that somebody else had used, or even to seem to have an association with the Southern Movement. So he continued to contend for the name Disciples. But in the main they came to be known individually as Christians while the corporate body was known as the Church of Christ. Raccoon John Smith stood up at the unity meeting between the followers of Campbell and Stone on January 1, 1832, at the Hill Street Church in Lexington, Kentucky and told the group that God has but one people upon this earth. God has given this people on the earth but one book, and the people should unite under one name on that book. This proposition seemed to solve their problem. Well, it would solve all of our problems today. This approach will solve all of the problems separating brethren. If everybody were to take the stand that Smith took regarding the one people of God, the one book of God, and the need to wear the same name we could find a basis for achieving unity.

It is unnecessary in this study to pursue the matter further. The difficulties the early restorers faced and fought out are clear and, alas, in many cases are still a part of our own experiences today. But thanks be to God for the toils they underwent and prevailed. Our task is much easier than the way through which they made their slow trek. Greater should be our appreciation for these early restorers, for the church of our Lord which they restored. Because of them you and I can be members of the church of Christ.

We can and should wear the name of Christ. If any have rejected the name of Christ and become entangled with denominationalism, they ought to come out of the institutions and stay out of them for the rest of their lives. We ought to become members of the church of Jesus Christ and serve Him through the church as long as we live or until He comes again.

Unto Him should we give glory in the church, by Jesus Christ, world without end. Blessed be the name of the Lord!

CHAPTER FOUR

BARTON WARREN STONE AND CANE RIDGE

Many people would expect to begin a study of the Restoration Movement with a consideration of the work of Thomas and Alexander Campbell. As a matter of fact, many historians do begin a study of the movement with Alexander Campbell. However, the truth of the matter is Barton W. Stone actually predates the involvement of the Campbells and has made a deep and indelible historical imprint. Thanks to Stone, the Restoration Movement was well on its way in Kentucky long before the Campbells came to America. Thomas came in 1807 and Alexander came in 1809. By that time Stone had already made his influence felt. In 1804 he converted the Cane Ridge Church, a Presbyterian church in Bourbon County, Kentucky into a Church of Christ. It was not until 1812 that Thomas and Alexander Campbell established old Brush Run Church in Brooke County, Virginia. So when discussing the Restoration Movement, one should strive to put into proper perspective the events, the individuals, and their contributions.

The congregation at Cane Ridge had been established in 1791 as a Presbyterian church, but it declared its identity with the New Testament Church in 1804 under the influence of Barton W. Stone. By 1811, Stone and Reuben Dooley were traveling throughout the western frontier of Kentucky, Southern Ohio and Tennessee doing what Stone termed "strengthening and founding churches." During this time that he was preaching and establishing other congregations after the New Testament order, Alexander Campbell and his father were identified with the Washington Christian Association, which was not the church in any sense of the word. Therefore, it seems fair and accurate to consider Stone and his work, along with that of his associates, as being previous to the Campbells' efforts to advance the Restoration Movement, particularly on the western frontier. Some have rightly styled it the Stone-Campbell Movement.

Let us now turn our attention to Barton Warren Stone. The "Warren" in his name was the family name of his mother. Mary Warren married John Stone and they gave their son the name Barton Warren. He was born in Tobacco, Maryland, on Christmas Eve of 1772. His father died when he was a three-year-old lad, and his mother bundled up the entire family, seven in number, and all of their slaves, and moved to Virginia. When Mary made that long trip from Maryland into that part of Virginia which borders North Carolina, she indeed represented the courage and bravery of a true pioneer woman. The mother of Barton Stone might well have been the model of the statue of the pioneer woman which is located in Ponca City, Oklahoma, to remind all who see it of those gritty females who drove covered wagons into the Oklahoma territory. Mary Stone was a staunch role model for her son.

Little is known about the religious orientation of Barton's father, John. However, it is known that his mother was a communicant of the Church of England. Later, after the family had moved to Virginia, Mary left the Episcopal Church and joined the Methodist Church. Barton himself was sprinkled as an infant, involuntarily submitting to what was called "baptism" or "christening" by an Episcopal priest named Thomas Thornton.

As a young man Stone displayed few religious inclinations. In fact, he had become greatly confused, astonished, astounded, and more than a little discouraged by the controversies and the conflicts that he had heard as they were found among the Episcopalians, the Baptists, and the Methodists. These were the denominations most prevalent in his early days. So he decided to give his attention to more worldly matters. Early in his life he was infatuated with the politics of Virginia, the state known as the "Mother of Presidents." A large number of the early Presidents and other leaders of our country came from Virginia—more than from any other state in the Union. Some of the early political leaders were ancestors of Barton Stone, so he was naturally drawn to the political arena and to the study of law, hoping to emulate some of his more illustrious ancestors by participating in state and federal governments. How to manage financially during the years of completing his education was a large practical concern.

Now Stone's father had provided that probation of his will and settlement of the estate would be delayed until the youngest, Barton, reached the age of twenty-one. However, because of financial obligations, the family decided to probate the will and settle the estate when Barton was only fifteen or sixteen years old. One might suspect that the older children also were eager to lay hands on their shares of the estate and not willing to wait until Barton became twenty-one. His obsession with learning and studying prompted him to consent to their wishes. Burning with a desire to move on in pursuit of his personal goals, he saw the settlement as an opportunity to advance his education. So on February 1, 1790, at the age of 18, he took his money and made the first step toward fulfilling his dreams.

Barton took his holdings and made the journey from his mother's home to a place near Greensboro, North Carolina, where he enrolled in the Guilford Academy. Nearly every institution of learning in that day was called either an academy or a seminary. But many of the historians, writing of the educational institutions, called them "log cabin colleges." Indeed, that is what Guilford really was. The President of the school lived in the upper-story quarters, and classes were held on the lower floor. This log cabin college was overseen and directed by a man named David Caldwell who was one of the outstanding educators of his day. He was a graduate of Princeton University. Such able and well-prepared educators were scarce on the western frontier, especially those who had graduated from such a distinguished university as Princeton and had chosen to teach in a frontier institution. Caldwell possessed multiple talents. He was a type of a "Renaissance Gentleman." In addition to being an accomplished educator, he was a physician, a Presbyterian preacher, and a successful farmer.

Most significant with respect to his influence on young Barton Stone, Caldwell was a Calvinist preacher. That is how preachers were identified in those days. They were either regular Calvinist or hyper-

Calvinist which denoted that they were more imbued with Calvinism than the regular Calvinists were. He believed in the Westminster Confession of Faith, and he accepted the doctrine that was set forth in that confession of faith. It was customary for Caldwell, because of his intense commitment to the religious training of his students, to bring to the campus outstanding Presbyterian preachers of the day. They would come to the school and conduct revival meetings or recommitment services and exert strong efforts to arouse the young men to a greater enthusiasm for matters of religion.

One of the prominent ministers who was invited to come to the campus was James McGready, a person to be remembered because of the impact he had upon the life of Barton Stone. McGready was a hyper-Calvinist. Stone went to hear him preach. What he heard, expertly delivered, was Calvinism. When McGready would call upon the audience to repent, Stone said that he made the plea so clear, plain, and so moving that it was as though he held sinners out over the fires of hell; captivating listeners could almost smell their very skin sizzling! McGready's presentation did not entirely appeal to Stone, though, for he could not reconcile in his own mind the concept of foreordination and predestination. He argued as he read his Bible that if a man is foreordained and predestined to salvation and the number is so fixed that it cannot be changed, then there is no need to preach to him; he is already saved and cannot be lost. God has ordained salvation to him; he is of the elect. And, on the other hand, if the remaining half is ordained to damnation, there is no need to preach to them either, for they are already condemned and the number so fixed that talking to them about repentance is not only vain but cruel. Because of his inability to reconcile this doctrine with the Bible, he fell out with the kind of preaching that McGready was doing.

At a later date, a young man named William Hodge came to the campus, and instead of preaching in the fashion of McGready, Hodge preached on the subject "God is love." Well, Stone had never heard that approach before! Nobody had ever told him that God is love and that God loves everyone and that "He gave His only begotten Son that whosoever believeth in Him should not perish, but have everlasting life" (John 3:16). He just could not conceive of the love of God as being so vast that everyone has a chance to be saved and nobody has to be damned, and nobody has been saved without the possibility of apostasy. So, after listening to Hodge, he went out in the woodlands and prayed that night, asking God to forgive him for having wasted so much time listening to religious errors instead of seeking to find the

54

truth in the Bible as it is in Jesus Christ. From this point in time Stone turned his attention to an intense study of the Bible. William Hodge had motivated him to study to find out about God and about the true nature of faith and obedience.

But Stone was not much impressed in his early days with the ministerial students at Caldwell's school. He perceived them to be an odd bunch of people! He simply did not find fellowship or compatibility among them at all. He still had his mind set on studying law and going into politics. So he finally made the decision to leave Caldwell's log cabin college and go over to Hamden-Sidney Law School in Virginia. But on the day and night before he was to leave and set out for law school, there came one of the most violent storms that he had ever witnessed. For a day and night it rained so hard, the wind blew so strong, and the storm was so intense that everyone was confined to his room, and nobody could leave the campus. Stone took the storm to be an omen from God and a clear message that God did not want him to study law, but wanted him to stay at Guilford and become a Presbyterian preacher. He shared his thoughts with Caldwell and after their conversation, he was convinced that the storm had indeed been an omen from God. God had sent this storm to stop him in his tracks. He should go no farther. So he decided to stay and prepare himself for the Presbyterian ministry.

Completion of the four-year course at Guilford Academy took Stone only three years. By the time he had completed the course requirements, he had committed himself to preach. He found out in 1793 that, in order to preach for the Presbyterian Church, he had to be licensed, and eventually ordained. So Caldwell directed Stone to the attention of Henry Patillo, a leading representative of the Orange Presbytery in North Carolina. Stone arranged to go and take the examination for licensure to meet the requirement for the ministry. However, the very thought of subjecting himself to such a test frightened him to the core. Undoubtedly, the examination would include questions regarding the Westminster Confession of Faith, and since he had rejected some of the rituals and doctrines of the Presbyterian faith, he was afraid that his mind-set would hinder him in passing the examination and a license would be denied him. Patillo assured Stone, however, that he would conduct the examination in such a way that Stone would be able to pass it without trouble. And so it turned out successfully.

After passing the examination, Stone learned that there was a six-month waiting period before his license would be issued. While he waited, he decided to go to Washington, Georgia, where one of his brothers lived. Upon arriving there, he learned of a teaching vacancy in the Academy, and his brother arranged for him to get the job.

During the year he taught at the Washington Academy and, as Providence would have it, the principal was a young man named Hope Hull who had been exposed to the "Christian Connexion" advocated by James O'Kelly, Rice Haggard, and Clement Nance in North Carolina and Virginia. In addition to his work at the Academy, Hull was also riding the circuit among the Republican Methodist churches in the area. Stone accompanied Hull on his circuit rides and heard many of his sermons, lectures, and discussions. These experiences had a lasting effect upon Stone. He was beginning to see a light at the end of the tunnel which had been lit by O'Kelly, Haggard, and Nance and which had finally resulted in the establishment of the "Christian church."

Stone stayed in Georgia for a year, and then decided to return to North Carolina to claim his license. With his new license to preach in his possession, he decided that he would start preaching in the poor, rural sections of Western North Carolina. However, his heart was not in preaching. Consequently, people did not respond to his preaching with open minds. They did not have the same readiness of mind to hear Barton Stone that the Bereans had to hear the apostle Paul. Stone became greatly discouraged. His depressed state led to the decision to quit preaching in North Carolina and move to Florida.

Again Providence intervened. As Stone was making his journey from North Carolina toward the Florida border, he stopped at a little Presbyterian church to worship. And in the audience that morning was a woman whom he knew, one that he described as "a pious little old lady." She recognized Stone and began to inquire of his plans—what he was going to do and where he was going. When he answered her questions, she chided him, calling him a Jonah.

"You are just running away from a responsibility to God as Jonah did," she told him, "and you may get swallowed by a whale if you aren't careful. You ought to go to Tennessee and Kentucky to preach the gospel instead of going to Florida."

Well, her words had an effect and he decided to change his plans and his course; he would not go to Florida after all, but rather he would make his journey into Tennessee and Kentucky. As he made his way across Tennessee stopping here and there to preach, he passed near the city of Nashville. Though it is today the "Athens of the South"— the great city of learning—what Stone saw then was very different. He observed a poor "little village of about three hundred people—a settlement hardly worth noticing." (He probably did not know that five years before, Andrew Jackson had moved to Nashville, deeming it promising enough for him to establish a political base which was to send him to Washington and the Presidency of the United States.)

Stone traveled on through Tennessee preaching as he went and in the fall of 1796, he reached central Kentucky. Upon arriving in Kentucky, he applied to the Transylvania Presbytery for a preaching assignment. He presented his license and told the Presbytery that he had been licensed by the Orange Presbytery in North Carolina and wanted to preach at a place determined by the Presbytery. So Stone was assigned to the Cane Ridge Church in Bourbon County and to the Concord Church in Nicholas County. They referred to him as the "supply pastor." The reason for this term was a vacancy in both pulpits, and Stone was to "supply" until a permanent preacher could be appointed.

The cause of the vacancy was somewhat unusual. The Transylvania Presbytery and the Kentucky Synod had expelled the preacher, Robert Finley, because of drunkenness. The minutes of the old Presbytery and Synod make interesting reading. The record describes efforts to fire Finley because he had become a drunk. Strangely, his fall from grace may have been precipitated by a sanctioned practice of the church. It was not unusual for a preacher on the frontier to be paid for his services with farm produce—such as chickens, eggs, vegetables and fruits. In some instances, the brethren paid the preacher with whiskey, and then they would fire him if he drank it! Human actions, even in religion, are sometimes hard to understand and reconcile. At any rate, Finley was expelled for drunkenness and Stone, as a result, got his job. In those days, it was not terribly unusual to find a preacher identified with strong spirits because Bourbon whiskey was distilled first by a Baptist preacher in Kentucky!

The situation which the new "supply pastor" found himself in at Cane Ridge and Concord is certainly worthy of consideration. Relics and records remain of the time that he was there. The building at Cane Ridge still stands. I preached there first in 1945 and many times since. The one at Concord was blown away by a cyclone a few years ago, after which the members moved into Carlisle and took membership in the churches there. The Cane Ridge Presbyterian Church was organized in 1790, and the old log meeting house was built in 1791, one year before Kentucky became a Commonwealth and was admitted to the Union. The year 1791 was a long, long time ago. This little one-room log meeting house was built right in the middle of the cane-brakes—hence the name "Cane Ridge." This was an area where the buffalo had roamed. In this area, the Indians had come to hunt the buffalo. They either had so many violent encounters among themselves or so many face to face confrontations with the white settlers who had moved there, that the land came to be known as the "Dark and Bloody Ground." Cane Ridge Church was built right in the middle of that ridge. The building has been recognized for its historical significance, and rightly so; but it is much better known for the role which the congregation played in the Restoration Movement.

The first group that came from North Carolina and Virginia to settle in that area of Kentucky did so at the suggestion of Daniel Boone. There is apparently no evidence that Daniel Boone was influenced by the Restoration Movement, but a brother and a sister did become identified with the movement. His sister, Hannah, joined John Mulkey in Monroe County near Tompkinsville, Kentucky, in restoring a New Testament Church. She died there, and her grave and stone are in the old Mulkey Church cemetery. So Daniel Boone was interested in friends, interested in their coming to Kentucky, interested in their settling on Cane Ridge.

The first preacher at the Cane Ridge Church was Andrew McClure. Most historians list Robert Finley as the first, but it was Andrew McClure who first preached there. However, he died when he was only twenty-seven years old, so he had little time to make a lasting contribution.

McClure was followed at Cane Ridge by Robert W. Finley, who lived to be ninety years old. While Finley resided in the community, he organized a seminary. He was a great educator, and three of the people who signed the Last Will and Testament of the Springfield Presbytery were students in his school. So here we find right in the middle of the cane brakes, in the heart of Bourbon County, Kentucky, individuals establishing a permanent settlement. One of their first moves was to organize this little Presbyterian Church. When Stone came to Kentucky, he came bearing a license from the Orange Presbytery, but he had not yet been ordained. Even a casual study of the religious organizations of that day reveals that the Presbyterians required the highest level of education possible before they would ordain one to the ministry. Stone qualified academically to be ordained, but the Presbytery had to examine him before they were willing to ordain him. His license was limited, so they would not ordain him on the basis of it alone. Again, Stone suffered the secret fear that had haunted him before the examination for licensure that his peers would expose his doubts about Presbyterian doctrines. He shared his reservations with James Blythe and Robert Marshall, who were scheduled to examine him at the ordination ceremony. He told them of his concern over being asked questions regarding the Westminster Confession of Faith, in which he had so little faith. He had doubts, especially concerning the doctrine about the "Trinity" as taught in the confession. He also questioned the doctrine of election, the doctrine of foreordination and predestination, and the doctrine of the perseverance of the saints. He could not harmonize the tenets of the confession with the teaching of the Bible. He told his examiners that if they asked him about these things, he would be forced to publicly renounce the creed and doctrine. But Blythe and Marshall assured him that they would conduct the examination in such a manner that he could meet the requirement which would enable them to ordain him. He underwent the same ordeal through which every other young Presbyterian preacher in America had gone. They were not handling his case in a different way. They simply would not allow him to preach on a permanent basis until he had been ordained by the ecclesiastical bodies known as the Presbytery and Synod. On October 4, 1798, the Presbytery met in the Cane Ridge Church house for the sole purpose of ordaining Barton W. Stone as a Presbyterian minister. They studied his status and the situation with which they were dealing and Blythe and Marshall agreed to ask him this question: "Do you receive and adopt the Westminster Confession of Faith as containing the system of doctrine taught in the Bible?" Well, what about that? They didn't ask him one thing about what he believed the Bible taught. They wanted to know what he believed about the Confession of Faith and whether the Confession of Faith contained the same system of religion that was revealed in the Bible as New Testament Christianity. Why would an examiner ask that type of question to a petitioner for ordination? Today we are not concerned about what a creed teaches. The fact is that creeds have become an albatross. If a creed teaches less than the Bible, it is a dangerous thing. If it teaches more than the Bible, it is a very dangerous document to accept. But if it teaches the same thing as the Bible, we do not need it! The solution to the matter appears clear and simple: abolish the creed and take the Bible only. Stone saw when he was asked this question that he had won the victory, so he answered loudly enough for everyone in the meeting house to hear him.

He said, "I do, insofar as I see it consistent with the Word of God."

Well, who among us cannot say that in complete honesty and with a clear conscience? "If a human creed is consistent with the Word of God, I will take it though I do not need it. If it is not, I will not accept it. I would advocate the Westminster Confession of Faith if it were consistent with the Word of God. If it were not, I would reject it as Stone did." Well, either Blythe and Marshall did not know what to do with him following that kind of answer or they were satisfied with the answer he had given. They straightway ordained him as the minister of Cane Ridge and Concord Churches.

This experience was a turning point in the religious life of Barton Warren Stone. It was also a turning point in the status of the Cane Ridge Church, for Stone said from that time on, he made the Bible his constant companion and turned away from the rites and the rituals of the Confession of Faith. He took the Bible with him when he went out to the fields to plow. He took the Bible with him when he went to milk the cows and feed the hogs. He took the Bible to the field when he was harvesting his crops. The Bible became his constant companion, and he pored over its pages and studied it as he had never before studied any subject.

It was about this time that a great awakening—a great religious awakening—swept over the western frontier. Its influence was felt in Kentucky, Tennessee, Alabama, Missouri, Indiana, Georgia, North Carolina, Virginia and Ohio. A great religious awakening it was because the people on the frontier had not been a very religious folk. They were void of convictions, and in many cases they were downright anti-religious. This great awakening was promoted by what one would call surges of revivalism and evangelism. The preachers simply began to preach everywhere, all of the time, and people would come together in great numbers to listen to the preaching. Revivalism and evangelism were contrary to the system of the Westminster Confession of Faith since Presbyterian churches did not evangelize under that system, nor did they conduct revivals. There was, after all, nothing that could be done about the non-elect. There was nothing needed by the elect. So why conduct revivals? Eventually the Presbyterian Church divided over that very issue, and the seceding branch came to be known as the Cumberland Presbyterian Church. Stone, however, just plowed right down the middle. He did retain his identity with the regular Presbyterian Church. He did not go with the Cumberland Presbyterians, but he became engaged in preaching and exhorting as part of this great awakening. Richard McNemar wrote a book about seven revivals which took place in Kentucky and Southern

Ohio. We have been proned to think that the only revival which took place was at Cane Ridge. Well, an important one did take place there, but not the only one! McNemar documents the fact that there were actually seven. They were all significant. But the other six, the fact remains, were mostly waves on the surface when compared to the one at Cane Ridge in August 1801, which rightly became the most noted of them all.

James McGready by this time had joined the revivalist movement and moved away from hyper-Calvinism of foreordination and predestination. He had been so offensive by his preaching in North Carolina, that some of his enemies drove him out of the state and burned his pulpit. He then moved to Logan County, Kentucky in 1798 and was assigned engagements by the Presbytery to several places in that county. He preached at the Red River Presbyterian Church, Gasper Creek Presbyterian Church, and the Muddy River Presbyterian Church. He began to preach what he was preaching in North Carolina, with the result of turning the Kentucky community upside down, and that in a short time. He aroused the greatest enthusiasm in the revivals and stirred his audiences to the highest pitch. Stone heard about McGready's meeting and decided to go to Logan County to see and hear what was going on.

Raccoon John Smith, on hearing about McGready and his meeting, and passing through the area, had a different reaction. He was preaching for the Baptists in Wayne County, Kentucky at that time, but he was still a Calvinist under the dictates of the Philadelphia Confession of Faith, so he discounted all of the emotionalism that McGready was arousing and cultivating. He wanted to have little or nothing to do with the man or with what he was preaching.

Stone, however, followed up on his interest and went down to Logan County to see for himself what was happening. He went there in the spring of 1801 to attend one of the meetings which McGready was conducting. He was deeply impressed by what he heard and saw. "This kind of preaching will turn the religious world upside down," he thought. Still greatly affected, he went back to Cane Ridge, where he took the pulpit on Sunday morning to preach. Can you imagine what he took as his text? Mark 16:15-16! He preached his sermon on Mark's account of the commission that Jesus gave to His apostles: "Go into all the world and preach the gospel to every creature. He that believeth and is baptized shall be saved. He that believeth not shall be damned." Stone said he saw in that text proof that God was willing to save anyone who heard and believed the gospel. He concluded that

God has made salvation universal. He saw that every creature in all the world can hear and believe the gospel and be saved without direct and miraculous intervention by the Holy Spirit. Perceptive as he was, and eager as he was to drive home the great truths of the Bible, he failed to see baptism in that Commission at all. He made no mention of the requirement to be baptized. He was not at all impressed with baptism at that time because he was zeroing in on the fact that God would save an individual who believed the gospel and that an individual could hear and believe the gospel without the intervention of the Holy Spirit. Stone was refuting Presbyterian doctrine. Later he learned that there was more to the Commission than he had seen and he began to preach it in its entirety.

Now arrangements had been made during the summer of 1801 for an annual communion service to be held at the Cane Ridge Church in August. The Presbyterians of the region of Tennessee, Kentucky, Ohio, and West Virginia had announced an annual communion service and laid plans to attend as was typical of the Presbyterians of that day. They had acquired this practice from Scotland, and they were bent on repeating communion at Cane Ridge. Stone and his group made ready for the service. Shortly after the crowd began to gather a revival broke out. Six or eight of the clergy were preaching at the same time. There were 25,000 people camped on the campus of the Cane Ridge Church. They had arrived in wagons, buggies, on horseback, by walking, and by any mode of transportation that would get them there. Anyone who has visited Cane Ridge is astonished at the limitations of that site and wonders how 25,000 people could have been crammed into that place. Those who wrote about the revival at the time said this number was present, and Stone himself confirmed it. This revival was typically a denominational camp meeting. It was emotional to the very core. Many of the people were shouting. Many more were weeping. Many were falling down as if dead. Others were outside the building, holding onto trees and barking. All were hysterical. These emotional outpourings gave rise to what must have been a strange and dramatic scene. As he remembered the day, Stone recalled forty years later the scenes in vivid detail, even to the site where he stood and preached.

On his final visit to Cane Ridge which occurred in 1843, Stone pointed out to his host the very spot where the stand was where he stood and preached. This had been the experience of a lifetime. Methodists, Baptists, Presbyterians, and any others who would preach spoke to sections of this great crowd. Many made stump speeches or on logs, or from whatever stand they could erect. The revival lasted from August

7 to August 12. Some writers said that the reason the meeting closed when it did was because the community literally ran out of food, forcing the hordes of people to go home. Now from that point in time, Barton Warren Stone and his associates began to preach the pure and simple gospel of Jesus Christ, free from all the trappings and the hindrances of confessions of faith. Such was the momentous and far-reaching effect of the great Cane Ridge revival.

The associates of Barton Stone, though perhaps overshadowed later by Alexander Campbell, deserve consideration to the highest degree. He was not out on a limb by himself. He was not a Goliath or a David fighting for the whole army. He was not out there making declarations and affirming propositions all by himself. There was a group of Presbyterian preachers who became closely affiliated with Stone in Kentucky and Ohio. Robert Marshall was the oldest of the group. At this time Marshall was preaching at the Bethel Presbyterian Church in Fayette County, about eight miles west of Lexington, Kentucky. Born in Ireland in 1760, he came to America with his widowed mother the same year that Barton Stone was born. So he was about twelve years older than Stone. He fought in the Revolutionary War and was engaged in the battle of Monmouth. Marshall was educated in Virginia and Pennsylvania and was licensed to preach by the Red Stone Presbytery in Pennsylvania. He came to Kentucky in 1791, the year that the Cane Ridge meeting house was built, but he was assigned by the Transylvania Presbytery to the Bethel Church. Marshall died on June 16, 1832, and was buried in the church cemetery.

Two other individuals associated with Stone at Cane Ridge were Richard McNemar and his brother-in-law, John Dunlavy. McNemar came to Kentucky from Pennsylvania and was licensed to preach by the Transylvania Presbytery in 1794. He was licensed "to exhort not oftener than once in two weeks and not to exceed 40 minutes in length." How would preachers feel today if they were told to exhort only once every two weeks, for forty minutes or less? Well, the Presbytery assigned McNemar to the Cabin Creek Church in Lewis County. John Dunlavy was granted a probationary license to preach by the Transylvania Presbytery on January 4, 1797. He was ordained on November 7, 1797, by the Presbytery and "set apart to the holy work of the gospel ministry by prayer and by laying on of hands." That was the regular ordination ceremony. Those in charge of the service had a prayer and placed their hands on Dunlavy. He was then assigned to the Eagle Creek Church in Brown County, Ohio.

The fourth associate was John Thompson. He went to Kentucky from North Carolina. He had been licensed to exhort by the West Lexington Presbytery in 1789. He was not licensed to teach, he was not licensed to preach doctrine, but only to exhort. His total responsibility was to exhort people after others had preached and had taught them what they should do. He moved in 1800 from Kentucky to Ohio, where he was eventually ordained by the Washington Presbytery and assigned to the Springfield Presbyterian Church.

The last associate of Barton Stone to be considered here was David Purviance, who was a ruling elder in the old Cane Ridge congregation when Stone arrived in 1796. The eldership was divided into at least two classes, one of which was called the "ruling elders." Purviance qualified as a ruling elder. He was a very distinguished Kentuckian. He served in the House of Representatives with great distinction and favorable attention. Purviance left Kentucky and moved to Ohio, where he was elected to the House of Representatives and the State Senate. He distinguished himself not only as a restoration preacher, but also as a statesman. More significantly, Purviance was one of the first individuals among this group to be baptized by immersion by Stone. All of these leaders had been sprinkled as infants. Purviance requested that Stone baptize him in old Stoner Creek, a stream running north of Paris, Kentucky city limits. Stone baptized Purviance before he himself had been immersed. Stone did not believe at the time strongly enough in immersion to teach its practice, but Purviance did.

Of the leaders who worked with Stone in the furtherance of the Restoration Movement, Thompson, Dunlavy, and McNemar had attended the log cabin seminary near Cane Ridge which was conducted by Robert Finley, so they all had strong ties to the Restoration Movement in that area as well as with Presbyterianism. They were, therefore, in strategic positions to make great strides toward bringing about a return to the Word, and they were disposed to wield their considerable influence. As a result, following the Cane Ridge revival, McNemar and Thompson were called before the Washington Presbytery and charged with heresy. But they were guilty of nothing in the world other than preaching the Bible. They were calling men back to the Bible and advocating that they take the Bible as the sole rule of faith and practice. Yet, the Washington Presbytery called them to account and charged them with heresy! Their case was referred by the Washington Presbytery to the Kentucky Synod, which was meeting at the First Presbyterian Church in Lexington, Kentucky on September 3, 1803. When the charges were read against Thompson and McNemar, the rest of their associates knew that if they were proven guilty the others would be brought to account under identical accusations. So they decided that they had better withdraw from the Synod while they could, or they all would surely be expelled.

Now one of the interesting footnotes pertains to Robert Marshall, who was secretary of the Kentucky Synod. He left his chair as secretary and joined the other individuals who had protested against the charges. When he asked to be heard, the Synod firmly denied his request. Instead of listening, the Synod began to prepare a case against the accused and shortly thereafter served notice of their expulsion from the Presbytery and the Synod. Furthermore, their pulpits were straightway declared vacant. The Synod then named a committee to go to all of the Presbyterian churches where these men had been preaching and notify them that their pulpits had been vacated. They would no longer be allowed to preach under the authority of the Synod and the Presbytery. There were fifteen of these congregations, eight in Kentucky and seven in Ohio. The result was that every last one of these congregations decided to renounce their allegiance to the Westminster Confession of Faith and to sever all affiliation with the Presbyterians. Every single one of these fifteen churches adopted the ancient order and the New Testament pattern.

What a dramatic and unexpected turn of events! And what courage shown by those champions of the Word as sole authority in matters religious and spiritual. However, Stone was not as convinced as most of the others were that leaving the Presbytery and the Synod was the right thing to do. So he made an appeal to the Presbytery and the Synod to allow the creation of a new Presbytery, with these fifteen churches to be affiliated with the Kentucky Synod. As one can imagine, and as Stone himself probably anticipated, denial of this request was immediate. The Synod would create its own Presbytery as it deemed fitting; it certainly would not delegate the task to a group of heretics!

Nevertheless, Stone and his associates proceeded in the fall of 1803 to organize what they called the Springfield Presbytery with these fifteen congregations as members. However, within less than a year, they realized that what they had formed was just as sectarian, fully as denominational and tainted by party spirit as the Transylvania Presbytery and the Kentucky Synod ever were. They were aghast to realize that what they had done was what they had been condemning all along. They had saddled themselves in ecclesiastical bondage that had no scriptural right to exist. So, on June 24, 1804, delegates met at the Cane Ridge meeting house, this time to abolish the Springfield Presbytery and write its Last Will and Testament. Now everyone who has not read the Last Will and Testament of the Springfield Presbytery should go to a library, find a copy, and read it. The document is basic and sets forth in clear terms the great plea of the Restoration Movement as perceived by Stone and the other signers. Richard McNemar is thought to have written most of the Last Will and Testament, but all agreed to sign it, and all did sign their names to the Will. Stone said that the document did not meet with all of their approbation, but none present saw any reason to reject it.

About this time Rice Haggard and his brother David migrated from North Carolina to Kentucky. Because Rice had heard about what was going on in the Stone camp, he made his way to Cane Ridge and, more than likely, influenced greatly the writing of the Last Will and Testament. He convinced Stone and his group, just as he had convinced James O'Kelly at the Lebanon meeting house in Surrey County, Virginia in 1794, that they ought to call themselves Christians. They decided to call themselves Christians and to call the congregations churches of Christ.

Now, apparently, all things were going well. They had the situation well under control and could see that they were making progress. They did indeed solidify this great movement, but the rejoicing was all too brief, lasting only about a year. Two disciples of the Shakers came from New York down to Brown County in Ohio and to Bourbon County in Kentucky to prey on those who had broken away from denominationalism and sectarianism. They sought to incorporate them as a part of the Shaker Movement. The Shaker preachers spent some time with Stone, but to no avail. They then went to Ohio and put the proposition to McNemar and Dunlavy, who fell for it. McNemar and Dunlavy agreed to leave the Stone movement and join the Shaker movement. (Two Shaker colonies, now defunct, were built in Kentucky: one at Pleasant Hill over in Mercer County near Harrodsburg, the other in Logan County, near Russellville.) There is reason to believe that McNemar and Dunlavy were the most radical in the Restoration group and they became easy prey for the Shakers. They were good fodder for the Shakers; they were virgin soil in which the Shakers could sow their seeds. Stone said that Dunlavy died in Indiana, raving in desperation over his folly of forsaking the truth for "an old woman's fable." McNemar was at last dismissed by the Shakers in a miserable, penniless condition. Great potential sadly wasted! Folly indeed!

Stone grieved greatly over his colleagues' apostasy, but he recovered somewhat from his disillusionment and his grief at losing these two men from the cause when another turn took place in 1811. Robert Marshall and John Thompson decided that the Bible was too latitudinarian and that, therefore, they ought to write a creed setting forth more clearly the faith and practice of the Restoration Movement. They believed that the Bible contains so much information that the average reader cannot grasp it well enough to decide what he should do. Marshall and Thompson proposed to write down what they believed and what they should practice and that would be their creed. Stone and Purviance opposed this action. So a meeting was scheduled to be held in 1810 over at the Bethel Church, where Robert Marshall was the minister, to settle the matter. They met and talked, but no agreement could be reached. At last they agreed to meet the next year at Mt. Tabor in Fayette County, Kentucky, to debate the matter at greater length, in the hope of arriving at a logical conclusion which all would accept. Thompson and Marshall had composed a paper setting forth what they believed to be the creed which ought to be adopted. Barton Stone and David Purviance opposed writing and adopting a creed of any sort. When the question was finally put to a vote, the representatives present voted overwhelmingly to reject the human creed and to accept the Bible as their only rule of faith and practice. They would follow the Bible and the Bible alone. What if the outcome had been different? What if that assembly had said, "Yes, we need a creed?" What if they had declared, "We have never been happy since leaving the Westminster Confession of Faith or the Philadelphia Confession of Faith. We ought to write a creed for ourselves." Where would the church be today? Would there not have been a mighty battle later to throw off that creed? Yet, there are some members of the church today who act as if they think there is a need for a human creed to set forth the identity of the church, what it believes, and what it practices. Folly still!

The ranks of the restorers had become smaller. Few hands were left to labor for the restoration of the ancient order. In December 1811, Marshall and Thompson left the Restoration Movement and went back to the Presbyterian Church. They went back to the Presbyterians and were restored by the Kentucky Synod. Now with the defection of McNemar and Dunlavy to the Shakers and the return of Marshall and Thompson to the Presbyterians, the only Christian soldiers left in Kentucky of note were Stone and Reuben Dooley. David Purviance had moved to Ohio by this time. What loneliness Stone must have felt!

He must have imagined in his lowest moments that all of his friends had forsaken him, and his enemies were so much against him that they wanted to take his life. But he rallied so completely from that kind of numbing doubt that he and Reuben Dooley decided, following the deaths of their wives, to farm out their young children among the brethren and take to the road, preaching and establishing churches. Now, does not this spirit and decision evoke shades of the first century?

The New Testament Church fought opposition that came wearing many faces and forms—Judaism, heathenism, and myriad other alien characters. Yet they finally won the upper hand as the church in Jerusalem went out and established churches all over Asia and Europe. Well, that is precisely what Stone did. He and Dooley went everywhere preaching the Word. In 1814, Stone decided with his second wife that he would leave Kentucky and move to Goodlettsville, Tennessee because he was under the impression that his mother-in-law had promised him the family farm and he felt that it was time to go and take over the farm. After he arrived in Goodlettsville and discussed the matter with his mother-in-law, he learned that he had misunderstood what she wanted to do. She refused to let him have the farm. Stone, under those circumstances, had no choice but to pack up and return to Kentucky. Alas, his situation was yet to get worse. When he arrived back in Kentucky he discovered that he could not afford to buy his farm back at Cane Ridge for the owner's selling price, and he had no money above that which he had received in the first place. So he reluctantly turned away from Cane Ridge and moved his family to Lexington.

These apparent misfortunes were leading Stone toward greater works and momentous contributions of which he had never dreamed. After his return to Kentucky, he established the Lexington Hill Street Church in 1816. This was the first church during the Restoration Movement to be established in the city. Four congregations had been established in the county. In 1819, Stone left Lexington and moved to Georgetown. There he bought the home of Israel Boone, a nephew of Daniel Boone. In Georgetown he established a congregation and became principal of the Rittenhouse Academy.

By this time reports reached Stone's ears that restorers were performing similar work and teaching the same things in West Virginia, Pennsylvania, and Northeastern Ohio that he had been following in Kentucky, Tennessee, and Southern Ohio. Stone decided that the Christians of the Stone movement and those of the Campbell movement ought to get together. The preachers ought to share with each other their thinking regarding their pleas and their practice.

Stone and Campbell did not actually meet for several years after the Restoration began. Campbell went to Kentucky for the first time in 1823 to debate W.L. McCalla over at Washington in Mason County. Campbell rode horseback with Sidney Rigdon all the way from Bethany, West Virginia to Washington, near Maysville. Stone chose not to attend that debate because he may have looked upon it as a squabble between an eccentric Presbyterian preacher and a radical preacher identified with a Baptist Association. Stone had never seen Campbell until 1824, a year after the debate, when Campbell returned to Kentucky and visited Stone at his home in Georgetown. (His old home had been lost to us for generations, but a few years ago it was located and opened to the public for visitation).

When Stone and Campbell at last had an opportunity to talk, they were gratified to discover that, in the main, they stood in agreement. After a lengthy conversation, Stone said that they agreed on most matters, and their causes paralleled one another so well that they ought to be united. As a matter of fact, over at Millersburg in Bourbon County, Stone had established a congregation and Campbell's followers had established another congregation there as well. So, in close proximity, there was a group of reformers after the Campells' order and a group of Christians after the Stone order. Millersburg was a small town, so it was easy for each group to learn about the other. It was practically impossible for them not to do so. What they found out was that their views were pretty well the same. So the two congregations united and merged into one congregation after the ancient order of things.

While Stone was preaching at Georgetown, John T. Johnson was filling a pulpit at Great Crossing in Scott County. Johnson was a Campbell convert. Stone, of course, had come to accept the truth on his own. Stone and Johnson exchanged pulpits and found that they were preaching the same things and their congregations were practicing the same things. They later invited John Rogers and Raccoon John Smith to come over to Georgetown for a discussion with them. Smith was preaching at Mt. Sterling in Montgomery County, and Rogers was preaching at Carlisle in Nicholas County. Stone had converted Rogers, and Campbell had converted Johnson and Smith. These four brethren, representing the Reformers and the Christians, decided to call a meeting for Christmas Day in 1831 to talk over their differences and their similarities. As they exchanged ideas, they came to realize that there were far more similarities among them than differences. Because they felt that the four of them did not constitute a large enough segment of the movement to propose a merger of the Christians and the Reformers, they sent out a call for a larger number of preachers and elders to meet at Lexington in the Hill Street Church on New Year's Day of 1832. It was decided with Stone's consent that Raccoon John Smith would make the keynote address and set forth the purpose of the meeting, to consider uniting of the Christians and the Reformers. Barton W. Stone agreed to follow Smith, either to challenge what he said or to express agreement and recommend a course to be followed. Smith's speech delivered on that occasion is well worth reading today; there is much in it that is interesting and much that is relevant. It is a masterpiece of persuasive rhetoric as he set forth the basis for unity between these two groups. He said that God has but one people upon the earth and that God has given His people but one Book. He pointed out that in that one Book God commands His people to be one. When he finished, Stone arose and said that he had not one point of disagreement with what brother Smith had said. "I have here and now given him my hand," Stone declared, and the two men shook hands, an action meant to symbolize the unity of the two groups and the binding of them together in one body upon the one Book.

This meeting was undoubtedly one of the highlights of the Restoration Movement. Here, proclaiming their oneness in fellowship, were most of the dedicated preachers who were preaching the Bible and calling all men back to the Bible. They were practicing what the Bible teaches Christians to practice. The delegates to the unity meeting chose Raccoon John Smith and John Rogers to go among the restored churches to spread the good news of the unity meeting. John T. Johnson volunteered to raise the money from among the brethren to finance Smith's and Rogers' journeys. That was a great day of unity! The only way for unity to be achieved today is on the same basis that existed that day. There would be no division in the church today if we would just take the Bible as they took it, teach the Bible as they taught it, and practice what the Bible teaches to be practiced. Their guide in all matters was the Bible. This is the solution—the source of unity—for all in any age.

This blessed state of unity held for several years, until departures from Bible practices led to division within the movement. In 1849, an assembly of delegates met in Cincinnati, Ohio and voted to organize and affiliate congregations with the American Christian Missionary Society with Alexander Campbell as the president. The result of this action was to divide the restored churches right down the middle.

Some of them became society-churches, and some remained non-society churches. The society issue was a great hindrance to unity. Then, ten years later (1859), L.L. Pinkerton decided that the singing was so bad in the church at Midway, Kentucky that even the rats could not bear to stay in the meeting house while the congregation was singing. The rats in the house were scared away, he declared, with the screeching and squalling which the members called "singing." So he decided the church ought to introduce a melodeon to assist them in their singing. The introduction of mechanical instruments of music further divided the churches. Those who were affiliated with the missionary society in the main also introduced the organ. These innovations produced congregations which were missionary society-organ churches and the other congregations remained non-society and non-organ churches. This division among churches spread throughout the brotherhood and resulted in churches of Christ on one hand and Christian Churches on the other hand, both groups claiming to have roots in the Restoration Movement. The churches of Christ remained Biblical and became non-organ and non-society while the Christian Church took a position for the society and the organ. The Christian Church later divided into the Independent Christian Church and the Christian Church (Disciples of Christ). Both represent the aspects of denominations.

It would indeed be a grand occasion to celebrate if unity would be restored. If those who have rejected the authority of God's Word would lay aside their innovations and return to the ancient order of things, unity would obtain. May God hasten that day and forbid the further apostasy of others! Would it not be grand if the three groups which claim roots in the Restoration Movement would unite again as the one people of God upon the one Book which God has given to His people? How pleasant our times would be if the brethren everywhere would dwell together in spiritual unity!

CHAPTER FIVE
ALEXANDER CAMPBELL AND BRUSH RUN

An overview of Barton Warren Stone and the Cane Ridge Church which we have given is basic to any understanding and appreciation of the Restoration Movement. One cannot possibly overstress the importance of the roles that both played in this great movement to restore New Testament Christianity in America by turning strictly to the Bible. A similar overview of the Campbells, Thomas and Alexander, and the Brush Run Church on Buffalo Creek in Brooke County, Virginia, must accompany a study of Stone if one is to acquire a balanced, historically accurate, picture of the Restoration Movement.

A cursory consideration of Barton W. Stone and Alexander Campbell would lead most people to draw up a list of similarities. The two men are indeed subject to comparison to a great extent. But also to a great extent they present a vivid contrast, for they were two strong and distinct personalities, and they represented differences within the movement itself. Cane Ridge and Brush Run, the sites of two significant historic institutions, encourage comparison in many ways. But they also lend themselves to contrast because of the influence of Stone at Cane Ridge and the influence of Campbell at Brush Run.

Barton Stone and Alexander Campbell were different, both in their approach to what they were advocating and in their influence upon the people who came into contact with them. One of the reasons for their distinctive differences was that they came from entirely different backgrounds. Though heredity admittedly plays a great part in a person's development and direction, it is impossible to separate backgrounds and environments from the process of growth and development. It is "how we set our sails that determines the way we go." These two men represent significantly different backgrounds. Stone came from an isolated rural society in America. He was one among a large number of children who grew up as orphans. The father, with few, if any, deep religious convictions, died when Barton was three years old and the poor mother nurtured Barton and his six siblings as best she could in rural Virginia. Stone had little religious or financial support from his parents, while Alexander Campbell was nurtured by concerned parents, very pious, devout, and ever watchful over their son, both in Ireland and in America.

Stone and Campbell were strikingly unlike in personalities. Stone appeared to acquaintances and close friends as a quiet, unpretentious, lovable little fellow. He represented the very finest in a quiet and peaceful atmosphere of rural agricultural Bourbon County, Kentucky. Campbell, on the other hand, was more brash, egotistical, arrogant one as a rich farmer in Virginia. He was more confident in his beliefs, feelings and preaching than Stone ever was. His confident presentation stopped Stone in his tracks. For one thing, Stone said that it was Campbell who really taught him the full significance of baptism. Very few people have been successful in characterizing Alexander Campbell; only incompletely has anyone been able to describe his personality or to present him in a fair and unbiased light. One person is said to have been asked for a description of Campbell. He said, "The one thing that I would say about him is that his nose turns a little bit to the north."

Because of their contrasting backgrounds, personal traits, and approaches to preaching, their contributions to the Restoration Movement were made at different levels. Stone seemed content to labor at a regional level, and he launched out not very far from where he lived. He went into Clark County, Fayette County, Mason County, and some of the other adjoining counties, but he kept himself rather

74

limited so far as outreach and mobility. Not so with Alexander Campbell. He traveled from the north to the south and from the east to the west. He made treks from America to England, Ireland, Scotland, and anywhere else to which he was invited. He sailed down the Mississippi River to New Orleans intent on converting the citizenry of that colorful city, but he soon found that they were more interested in selling cotton and speculating on other commodities than they were in receiving the gospel. So he turned around and started back home. On the way, he stopped in Jackson, Louisiana for a short stay. He preached at the Episcopal Church, one of the oldest Episcopal churches in America. James Shannon was serving as president of Louisiana College in Jackson at the time. While Campbell was there, he converted Shannon and his wife and then persuaded him to go to Harrodsburg, Kentucky to become president of Bacon College. Shannon later went to Columbia as president of the University of Missouri. This was typical of Alexander Campbell, but it would have seemed presumptuous to Stone.

Once the influence of Campbell came to Kentucky where Stone lived, most of the Baptist preachers who were converted to the Restoration Movement in the early 1830's were converted as the result of reading the writing and hearing the debate of Campbell. Stone, however, seemed unwilling to let the influence of Campbell fence him in. When he concluded that Campbell was invading his territory, he packed up and moved to Jacksonville, Illinois (1834). There he lived for the last ten years of his life. An interesting story surrounds the death and burial of Stone. When he became seriously ill on a preaching tour, he went to the home of his daughter, Amanda, who lived in Hannibal, Missouri, with her husband, a colonel in the United States Army. He lingered there for a number of days with no signs of improvement. When he died, his body was shipped from Hannibal to Jacksonville and buried there in a locust grove on his farm. When his wife sold the farm, his casket was moved to the cemetery of the old Antioch Church, which he had founded as a Restoration Church in 1832. Later, the Cane Ridge Church of Christ took his body up once more, that is what was left of it after the onslaught of worms and time, and took it to the Cane Ridge Church cemetery for a third burial. Hopefully, he will be allowed to remain there until the Lord comes for him on that Great Day to raise him from the grave.

My close study of the Stone/Campbell movement has resulted in a warmer personal attachment to Stone than to Campbell, simply because of the nature of the two men. That matter, however, is ephemeral and incidental. Any consideration of the movement must give full credit to both; neither of the two can be left out or de-emphasized. But after all, Stone should be given first place in that he did come to the movement first. Campbell did not come to America until five years after Stone had introduced the plea and concept of the Restoration Movement and had already converted a multitude of people to the truth. But in studying their roles in the movement, one finds that they seemed to have devoted little attention in the early days, to the establishment of local congregations. They had a smattering idea of transforming Christendom into a system that would bear benchmarks of New Testament Christianity. Their labor in that direction was diligent and intense. It did not seem to dawn on them in the early stages of their work that what they were trying to accomplish must be translated into the operation of local congregations which represented Christianity and the whole system found in the Bible. They seemed to have devoted their time and effort to the proposition of forsaking and abandoning creeds and confessions of faith—an action which they claimed would bring about unity.

Well, that indeed was necessary; those creeds and confessions definitely had to be shed. They decided to clean out human creeds and confessions of faith from the hearts of men and plant the seed of the kingdom which is the Word of God. The hearers would no longer be any kind of sectarians. It finally dawned on Stone to convert the Cane Ridge Presbyterian Church in Bourbon County, Kentucky, to a church of Christ, but it took Thomas and Alexander Campbell until 1811 to decide that they ought to establish and organize the local congregation of Brush Run. Stone and Campbell decided to take as an example the Jerusalem Church as a local congregation and to also represent the universal church which was founded in A.D. 33. This is why the Cane Ridge Church played such an important role in the movement and why Brush Run played an equally important role. Both Stone and Campbell decided that the New Testament Church should be restored as a local congregation and become the pattern of what would happen during the Restoration Movement.

However, in the beginning they could not conceive of organizing local congregations of the church without setting up some sort of super-structure over all the congregations. Stone and Campbell had been so deeply seated in ecclesiastical organizations that they had difficulty in thinking of local congregations established here and there without some structure of an ecclesiastical nature to bring all congregations together. This mind-set likely accounts for Alexander

Campbell agreeing to be elected president of the American Christian Missionary Society in 1849 when it was formed in Cincinnati, Ohio. He simply believed in a system of organization for cooperation and decided on the missionary society to pull together all of the restored congregations. When Stone and his associates were expelled from the Transylvania Presbytery and the Kentucky Synod, they set about to establish a presbytery of their own that would include the fifteen congregations which had agreed with them. The result was the Springfield Presbytery organized in 1803. They could not conceive of having a local congregation that was not a part of a denominational and sectarian structure. Stone tried to get the Kentucky Synod to accept it as one of their Presbyteries, but the Synod would have nothing to do with it. A year later, however, six of the preachers voted to abolish the Presbytery and wrote its Last Will and Testament.

When Thomas Campbell came to America from Ireland in 1807, the North American Presbyterian Synod was meeting in Philadelphia. He presented his ministerial credentials and was assigned to the Chartiers Presbytery in Western Pennsylvania. The Chartiers Presbytery assigned him to four places in Pennsylvania to preach in Presbyterian churches. Thomas Campbell became a sort of circuit rider, preaching to and tending the flocks. Well, it was not long after he began to preach in these four places that he showed his true colors—colors which had begun to show in Ireland, where he had tried to get the Church of Scotland to reform itself. Failing in that effort, he finally joined the seceders and represented them when he moved to America. And so in Western Pennsylvania he began to preach the same things which he had decided in Ireland that he should preach. It was not long until he was called before the Presbytery and the Synod to account for what they called heresy. Of course, he denied that he was a heretic. He denied that he was violating the Scriptures in what he was preaching, but the powers were more interested in him preaching the tenets of the Westminster Confession of Faith than they were in him preaching the gospel of Jesus Christ. Campbell was called into account for violations of what the Confession required. The defense that he made before the North American Synod makes interesting reading, but it was not convincing enough to satisfy the Synod. So the Presbytery and the Synod declared his pulpits vacant and denied him the privilege of entering the pulpits of any of these four churches.

Well, what was he supposed to do now? A young preacher in a strange land who had lost his congregation. It is hard to understand why he did not think about just going ahead and establishing a church after the New Testament order. Instead, he decided with his associates to organize the Washington Christian Association. This was merely an association of Presbyterians who were in sympathy with Campbell. A meeting of this Association was held at Abraham Alters' home outside the city of Washington, Pennsylvania, and Thomas Campbell was called upon to deliver a sermon. In this speech Campbell used a phrase that has become the famous motto of the Restoration Movement. He said, "Where the Scriptures speak, we will speak, and where the Scriptures are silent, we will be silent." That was a pronouncement of the highest order! He meant that they were going to take the Bible as their only rule of faith and practice, and what the Bible says, they would teach and practice, and where the Bible is silent on any subject, then they would refuse to teach on that subject. They said in effect, "We will call Bible things by Bible names, and we will do Bible things in Bible ways." They proposed to unite all believers upon this principle.

Just imagine how shocking that announced course was to the assembled audience! They had never heard a thing like that said before. No one had ever said that before this side of the first century. And so there was not only consternation among the people, but there was also outright grumbling from some of the individuals. Andrew Monroe stood up and said, "If we follow what Campbell has recommended, that will be the end of the practice of infant baptism. Look what you have done. You have taken infant baptism away from us—a thing which we have all practiced." Monroe's words and the tears streaming down his face showed his admission at least that the Bible does not teach infant baptism. Thomas Campbell replied, "If it must go, it must go." Thomas Atchison stood up with tears in his eyes too and said, "The motto which you have just announced violates the Scriptures that quote Jesus as having said 'suffer these little children to come unto me and forbid them not, for to such belongs the kingdom of God.' You have cut out all of the children. What will we do with the children?"

Thomas Campbell said to the skeptics, "There is not a word which you have quoted from the Bible that says anything about sprinkling babies." Infant baptism was not what Jesus was talking about at all in Luke 18:16.

James Foster then stood up in the meeting and said in substance, "I will explain to all of you what I think baptism is. Baptism is, as the Bible teaches, a burial and *not a sprinkling or pouring process*. The act of baptizing includes water in a burial as a dead body is buried in the earth." He continued his figure by saying, "Dust is dust, and water is water, and when we die we are buried in the dust of the earth from which we came, and when we are baptized, we are buried in water with the Lord by baptism into his death and raised to walk a new life" (Romans 6:1-5).

By this time the Campbells were rapidly moving to separate themselves from denominationalism and sectariansim. Their progress can be seen in their reaching such conclusions as they found in the Bible. Now, soon after the Christian Association of Washington was formed, Campbell made application for membership into the North American Synod for the association. The Synod had never had that kind of application before. It was not unusual for Presbyterian churches to make application to the Synod, but no one had ever heard of this kind of situation where a maverick group was seeking membership in the Synod. They firmly replied, "We have no place for you. Your group will not fit in with us, and we will not fit your association."

Following the outright rejection by the Synod of the Association, Campbell turned his attention primarily to reforming the corrupt practices and the false teachings of the Presbyterian churches. That is why in the early days of the Restoration the Campbells were called reformers. They were not called disciples with a capital "D." They were more often called Christians. They were called Reformers because they had set out to reform what they found to be wrong among the denominations. Here is what Campbell said about the situation at that time:

> Is it therefore, because I plead the cause of the scriptural and apostolic worship of the church in opposition to the various areas and schism which have so awfully corrupted and divided it that the brethren of the unity should feel it difficult to admit me to their fellowship?

Was this, then, why the ecclesiastical authorities had rejected him? Was it because he showed them their false teachings and corrupt practices and called them back to the New Testament pattern? Well, of course, that is exactly why the Synod wanted nothing to do with the Campbells. Thomas had it well figured out; he understood the situation full well. Eventually twenty-one members of the Christian Association of Washington met with Thomas Campbell on September 7, 1809, and requested that he write and print a document which finally became his Declaration and Address. The Declaration and Address included statements which were highly relevant to the future of the Restoration Movement.

Two or three of the items in the Declaration and Address deserve our attention. Campbell asked, "Why should we deem it a thing incredible that the church of Christ in this highly favored country should resume that original unity, peace, and purity which belongs to its constitution?" Secondly, he observed that "the church of Christ upon the earth is essentially, intentionally, and constitutionally one." It is not divided up into denominations and sects. It is one body, for by one Spirit we were all baptized into one body and the Church is that one body. Thirdly, Campbell says, "nothing should be bound upon Christians as articles of faith or required of them as terms of communion, other than what is expressly taught and enjoined upon them in the Word of God." What does the Westminster Confession of Faith require? What does the Philadelphia Confession of Faith require? It makes no difference! There should not be bound upon an individual or a group of individuals anything that is not expressly taught and enjoined upon them by the Bible, the inspired Word of God. And finally, Campbell said with respect to the commands and ordinances of our Lord Jesus Christ, "Where the Scriptures are silent as to the express time or manner of performance—if any such there be—no human authority has power to interfere in order to supply the deficiencies by making laws for the church." Campbell is saying that where the Bible is silent, keep your mouth shut! That is, in essence, what he said. Don't speak if the Bible does not speak. Do not bind on the church anything that is not expressly represented in the Bible. We should not speculate on the time and the circumstances or the manner of performance without the Bible. Authority— now that is basic. If Thomas Campbell were here today and he made that same speech, many audiences would blurt out, "Amen, brother Campbell, amen!"

Well, when Alexander Campbell came to America, Thomas had already been here for two years. It is hard to imagine how one good man could get himself into so much trouble as Thomas had done. Alexander and family arrived on American soil in 1809. There is a story about their leaving Ireland and being shipwrecked and during that time Alexander attended the University of Glasgow in Scotland for a year. When the family finally reached America, they went to Washington, Pennsylvania where Thomas was residing. At that very time the Declaration and Address was being printed. In fact, the first galley sheets or proof sheets had just come off the press, and Thomas was very eager and proud to share what he had written with his son, Alexander. Campbell told the Lord while he was on the wrecked ship that if he lived through the wreck that he would preach the gospel all of the days of his life. Thomas handed the galley sheets to Alexander and he read them carefully and prayerfully. Alexander then said to his father that he must abandon and give up infant baptism and other practices for which it seems you cannot find an expressed precept or example in any of the books of the Scriptures. Did Thomas know what he had gotten himself into when he published the Declaration and Address? Alexander told his father that he must not only give up infant baptism, but there are many other practices within Christendom that he was going to have to give up because there is no authority for them in any book of the Scriptures.

Thomas gave serious thought to what his son had said. He replied, "If it be so, then it must be so. Whatever must go, must go; and we will see that it does!"

Difficulties and snags became the daily business of the Campbells. Whatever they attempted, they faced barriers. They were rebuffed at every turn. They finally turned their attention and efforts to the task of organizing the Brush Run Church.

Of course, other matters became involved in their lives. Alexander Campbell was elected as a delegate to the State Constitutional Convention to meet in Richmond, Virginia. He went as a representative of the non-slave owners and small land owners of North Virginia. He had not been at the convention long until he ran afoul with the big land owners and the slave owners of South Virginia. He found himself on the verge of despair in his association with these members of the convention. John Randolph was one of the delegates from South Virginia. On one occasion he was so incensed with Campbell's contention that he said, "Nobody can satisfy Alexander Campbell. He is against everything anyone else wants to do." Randolph said Campbell came to America and found no church that would satisfy him, so he established one of his own.

Of course Randolph was mistaken about Campbell's case. He did not establish a church of his own, but he did restore the Lord's church at Brush Run when he organized a local congregation according to the New Testament pattern. Campbell turned his attention entirely from the reformation concept to the restoration concept, and he built the Brush Run Church on the order of the one described in the Bible. He required of it only that which the Bible taught as was required in the New Testament congregations of the first century. On May 4, 1811, the associates of the Campbells met together to constitute the Brush Run Church. At the first meeting Thomas Campbell was selected as the elder. One would infer that Thomas was the only one qualified to be an elder, yet it is surprising that the church would have agreed to having only one elder when the apostles ordained elders in every congregation. The church then ordained Alexander as the preacher. They granted whatever authority they could bestow upon him as a minister of the gospel. Four other men were selected as deacons of the congregation. This congregation knew what it was to appoint and grant elders and deacons the oversight of the Brush Run Church. The Campbells followed the same pattern and process in other congregations which they later established. They also agreed to meet on Sunday of every week to observe the Lord's Supper. At the time the Campbells established the Brush Run Church they had not heard of Barton Stone and the Cane Ridge Church of Christ in Bourbon County, Kentucky.

The Brush Run Church met on Sunday morning, June 18, 1811, with all intent to observe the Lord's Supper. All participated except three members who refused to engage in the breaking of bread and the drinking of the fruit of the vine. Upon inquiry, Thomas Campbell learned that they refused to commune because they had not been baptized. They had considered themselves members of the Brush Run Church, but since they had not been baptized, they concluded that they were not eligible to observe the Lord's Supper. These three, Abraham Alters, Margaret Fullerton, and James Bryant insisted that Campbell baptize them. So on July 4, 1811, Campbell took these three candidates to Buffalo Creek and there immersed them. Now that was a perfect way for them to celebrate the Fourth of July! Freedom from sin! Liberty in Christ! Before that day Thomas Campbell had never immersed anyone. He had never even seen anyone immersed. How in the world was he going to go about baptizing these three candidates in Buffalo Creek? He seemed not to have thought about wading out into the water with them and baptizing them. He located a hanging limb or an arching root of a tree which extended out over a deeper hole of water in Buffalo Creek. He climbed out on that tree root and asked the candidates to stand beneath him. Then he grasped them, one by one, by the tops of their heads and asked them to squat. With these peculiar stances he doused them under the water. That was a most awkward way to baptize candidates. Was it a burial? Well, surely it was. They were immersed in water while standing. King Tut was buried standing up in his ancient tomb, so it must have been all right to baptize these individuals by this type of burial as long as they were covered by water. No instructions or examples indicate that a person must lie horizontal to be submerged in baptism. Surely baptism can be performed perpendicularly; at least, that is the way Campbell did his first one. Objections came from certain people who said this was not the way to bury people in baptism in the first place, and, in the second place, Thomas Campbell was not eligible to baptize anyone because he himself had never been immersed. Subsequently, the baptism of the other Campbells was brought into question, along with that of the thirty members of the Brush Run Church because not one of them had been immersed!

Alexander Campbell had been married about this time to Margaret Brown, whose father owned the farm and the mansion to which Campbell later moved and which still stands. He and Margaret were married on March 12, 1811, and on March 13, 1812, just one day over a year later, their first baby daughter was born. She was given the name Jane after Alexander's mother. Now the question of whether to sprinkle baby Jane began to worry the infant's parents. It must be remembered that Alexander had told his father in no uncertain terms, that infant baptism was contrary to the principles of the Declaration and Address and the Bible. Alexander spent the next year feverishly studying the Bible on the subject of baptism. He went to the original Greek, and he studied what everybody else had written on the subject. His study led him to the conclusion that baptism meant immersion and a burial in water. Further, he came to the conclusion that sprinkling of adults and infants was unscriptural. He found no scriptural authority for sprinkling—none whatsoever. In fact, he could not find sprinkling as a mode of baptism mentioned anywhere in the Bible.

Campbell concluded that if sprinkling and infant baptism were invalid then none of them had been scripturally baptized.

Alexander Campbell translated the New Testament into what he called the "Living Oracle" and every time the word baptize appeared in the King James version, Campbell translated it immerse. Even when he came to the reference made to John the Baptist, he translated it John the Immerser. His translation was rejected among the Baptists for after all, he had translated them out of a name! When Campbell took away the name "John the Baptist" and called the forerunner of Christ John the Immerser, he removed the only mention in the Bible of anyone being called a "Baptist." That is how keenly Campbell came to feel about baptism after he had learned the truth.

Since the people who were members of the Brush Run Church had not been baptized, the question had to be faced by all of them. They had not thought about baptizing one another at that point in time. That solution among the preachers occurred to them later. Barton

Stone said that all of the preachers in Kentucky baptized one another; and then all of the baptized preachers baptized their congregations. Campbell knew Mathias Luce, a very distinguished Baptist preacher who was also the moderator of the Baptist Association. He made a trip to see Mr. Luce and while there asked the Baptist preacher if he would baptize him. After their serious and lengthy conversation, Luce concluded that Campbell wanted to be baptized upon a confession of his faith in Christ by the authority of the Father, the Son, and the Holy Spirit for the remission of his sins. Luce told Campbell that he could not do that. His Baptist Association would not allow it. They would kick Luce out. They would withdraw from him. Luce did go on to tell Campbell that he could baptize him into the Baptist Church without any trouble. Campbell replied that he did not want to get into the Baptist Church because he had just come out of the Presbyterian Church and he did not wish to get back into another denomination. Campbell did not want to be baptized into the Baptist Church. What he earnestly wanted was to be baptized as the Bible teaches.

Finally, Luce agreed to go and talk with Thomas, Alexander's father, about the matter. They spent a whole night together talking about baptism and the next morning they all agreed to go down to Buffalo Creek and Mr. Luce would baptize them all. When they reached the creek, Luce went with the candidates into the water. He baptized Thomas and his wife, Jane; Alexander and his wife, Margaret; and Alexander's sister, Dorothea, who later married James Bryant, and a Mr. and Mrs. James Hansen. Other members of the congregation looked on the scene from the creek banks. One of the young men who was supposed to go into town and register for the War of 1812 was disturbed because he wanted to watch the baptism. As it turned out, there was time for him to go and register for the Armed Forces and get back for the baptizing because Alexander and Thomas spoke for seven hours. These people stood at the Brush Run Church of Christ on Buffalo Creek in Brooke County, West Virginia, oblivious to the existence of another congregation like theirs in all of America.

It was about this time that the Campbells began to look about for Associations or other ecclesiastical bodies which they could join. James Deforest Murch, an eminent historian, skewed his writing though in support of the practices of the Independent Christian Church. According to Murch, in all matters the "new church" daily examined traditional beliefs and practices in the light of the Scripture. The only authority they had to rely upon was the New Testament. So they studied the Bible daily, Murch said. He further pointed out that there was, in spite of their devotion and dedication, a certain loneliness attached to their "congregational independence" and the brethren yearned for fellowship with others of like mind and heart which cooperation Murch would endorse. They sought to find others like themselves. They questioned whether they could have fellowship with a brotherhood outside the local congregation. So the Campbells decided to take the Brush Run Church into the Red Stone Baptist Association in Pennsylvania. Their application for membership was accepted. They seemed to find greater compatibility among the Baptists than they had experienced among the Presbyterians.

Campbell had already abandoned the practice of infant baptism, a basic doctrine of Presbyterianism. The Brush Run Church had accepted immersion, which the Baptists were already practicing, so there was, on the surface, a greater chance for association with them. The Baptist Churches east of Washington, Pennsylvania, and west of the Allegheny Mountains along the Monongahela River had formed the Red Stone Association. The Association offered Brush Run membership, probably because of the influence of Mathias Luce, their moderator. However, Campbell at first resisted. He originally thought that there was no need for anybody except the local congregation as an organized unit. But in 1812, he took the matter before the Brush Run congregation, which voted to apply for membership in the association. In the fall of 1813, Campbell laid the matter before the Red Stone Association with the provision that the Association would honor the beliefs and practices of the Brush Run Church on certain Bible matters. The Association probably did not know what it was agreeing to, but they said they would. So, with that agreement, the Brush Run Church accepted membership in the Redstone Baptist Association.

On August 30, 1816, the association conducted its regular meeting at Cross Creek with Campbell as one of the speakers. It had been a long time since the day they had admitted Campbell and they had been reluctant to ask him to speak. Five years after admission, Campbell accepted an invitation to speak and gave his famous address which came to be known as the Sermon on the Law taken from Romans 8:3. Campbell said the Baptists did not know the difference between the Old and the New Testament. They were just as likely to go to the Old Testament to find the conditions of salvation as they were to go to the New Testament to discover what one must do to be saved. To say the least, the Baptist ministers were deeply offended by Campbell's sermon. So when the Association met at Peter's Creek in 1817, the Association was prepared to raise questions about the orthodoxy of

Thomas and Alexander Campbell. But since they could not get enough people to take a position on the accusation, they passed it over. However, the issue was not dead; there were those who were determined to keep the pot boiling. They put it on the back burner for the time being, but it was still simmering into another year. In the meantime, Campbell had organized the Wellsburg Church in the place to which his father-in-law had moved. Great attractions were there, so Campbell went over, preached the gospel, and organized the Wellsburg Church.

Campbell had become acquainted with two distinguished Baptist preachers at Warren, Ohio: Adamson Bentley and his brother-in-law, Sidney Rigdon. Campbell's acquaintance with these two preachers led them to invite the Wellsburg congregation into the Mahoning Baptist Association which had been formed in 1820. Campbell consented to bring the Wellsburg Church into the Mahoning Association, and it maintained its membership until the association was dissolved. Campbell opposed the dissolution of the Mahoning Association because he wanted to retain an ecclesiastical affiliation with a body above and beyond the local congregation. The Red Stone Baptist Association met for the sole intent and purpose of expelling Alexander Campbell and the Brush Run Church from membership, but he had beaten them to the draw. He had already left Brush Run and taken the Wellsburg Church into the Mahoning Association. So there was nothing for Red Stone to do except to lick their chops and pass on to something else.

At about this time Walter Scott came from England to America. He sailed from England and landed in New York in 1818. He stayed a year with his uncle in New York and then pressed on westward to Pittsburgh, Pennsylvania in 1819. In Pittsburgh he came into contact with a man named James Forester. Forester had built an academy and organized a congregation after the concept of the Restoration Movement in Scotland held by the Haldane brothers. Scott identified himself with Forester and accepted a teaching position in his academy. This arrangement made it possible for them also to study the Bible together. This Haldane preacher baptized Scott in the Monongahela River in which Forester was later drowned while swimming. Following the death of Forester, Scott took over his work in Pittsburgh, both in the church and the academy.

Scott attended the Mahoning Association meeting with the Campbells and all were deeply impressed with him and what he was doing. The Mahoning Association of Baptist churches asked Scott to represent the Association as an evangelist on the Western Reserve, which is the northeast quadrant of Ohio. He was to preach the Philadelphia Confession of Faith which the Associates considered to be the gospel. Scott went to the Western Reserve and preached the gospel of Christ instead of Baptist doctrine. Instead of preaching the Philadelphia Confession of Faith as the Association had intended him to do, he preached the Bible and soon he was baptizing people hand over fist. So great was his success that he reported to the next meeting of the Mahoning Association that he had baptized 10,000 people that year!

Scott's success was as astonishing to the Campbells as it was to everyone else. Alexander sent his father up to the Western Reserve to see what Scott was preaching. He wanted to know what it was that Scott was doing. Thomas came back to Bethany and reported that Scott was preaching what was in the Book and nothing else. Scott was baptizing people on the basis of faith, repentance, confession of Jesus Christ, and baptism for the remission of sins. Thomas Campbell reported that Scott was preaching and practicing according to the Word of God, so he and Alexander agreed that they would encourage him to continue without interference.

In 1830, there was discussion among the members as to whether they needed to continue an organization such as the Mahoning Association. John Henry made a motion at the 1830 meeting to dissolve the Association. The motion passed. Campbell was taken by surprise for he had not heard that the resolution was to be introduced. He mildly opposed the passage for he was reluctant to give up this ecclesiastical association with its created hierarchy. Walter Scott persuaded Campbell to keep his peace and refrain from offering any objection to the resolution, so he allowed it to pass without protest. It soon became obvious that Baptist churches were drawing away from their Association as the Presbyterian churches had withdrawn from their Presbyteries and Synods. Most of the denominations which withdrew from their Associations were content to become congregations of the church of our Lord and Savior Jesus Christ.

The chain of events in Nashville, Tennessee, will serve as an example. Jeremiah Vardeman went to Nashville in 1820 and established the first Baptist church in the city. In 1823, Phillip Sidney Fall went to preach for that Baptist church, and it was not long until Fall saw that the Association to which the church belonged was unscriptural. At his request, the congregation withdrew from the Association. Fall then asked them to take the Bible as their only rule of faith and practice, which they did. This was the first restored church of Christ in Nashville, coming out of the group which Vardeman had established in 1820.

Similar things happened all over Kentucky and Tennessee and throughout Pennsylvania, Ohio and West Virginia. Congregations of the Baptist faith withdrew from their Associations and declared themselves independent of any ecclesiastical body. They wanted to become the New Testament Church. The biography of Raccoon John Smith, written by John Augustus Williams and more recently revised by Everett Donaldson, shows Smith to be a classic example of many individuals who studied and preached themselves out of Baptist doctrine and into the doctrine of the New Testament. What Smith was doing in Kentucky was being done all over the country. The Restoration Movement was taking hold by 1830, and the Word of the Lord was spreading like fire in dry stubble. What was happening in America is the same thing that happened in Jerusalem, Judea, Samaria, Galilee, and the uttermost parts of Asia and Europe when congregations described in the Bible were established.

Alexander Campbell came to a point in time that he upstaged his father and all of their associates. Thomas Campbell died in 1854, while Alexander lived until 1866. He was not only overshadowing his father prior to 1854, but he was also outshining the leaders of the Stone movement. People seemed to be turning to Alexander Campbell as the spokesman and leader of the whole Restoration Movement. Campbell reveled in that sort of attention. It has been said that Campbell came to the Cane Ridge Church one time after 1847 and saw the tomb that had been erected to Stone in the cemetery there. The tombstone bears the words which praise Stone as "the distinguished reformer of the Nineteenth Century." Campbell is reported to have looked at that inscription and muttered that Stone was one of the distinguished reformers—just one of many. Campbell's meaning was easy to see that he himself must be considered among those distinguished reformers.

Alexander Campbell distinguished himself by reason of the fact that he became a prolific writer and successful debater as well as a great teacher and preacher. He built a cubicle out on the campus of his home and whenever he was on the premises he went there at four o'clock in the morning to study until late at night. He became an excellent editor. He edited the *Christian Baptist* from 1823 to 1830. He intended to call the journal *The Christian*, but Walter Scott advised him to reconsider because the people would not read it if he named it *The Christian*; but if he would call it the *Christian Baptist*, at least the Baptists would read it. Consequently, Campbell named the journal *The Christian Baptist.* In 1830 he discontinued publication of *The Christian Baptist* and started publishing *The Millennial Harbinger* because he believed that if everyone accepted the pleas of the Restoration Movement, there would be a millennium in this land—hence, the name of his new journal. He continued to publish the *Harbinger* until he died in 1866. When he died, his son-in-law, W. K. Pendleton, took over the journal and published it for a short time until it was discontinued. Campbell had also published the debates in which he engaged as well as other books which he had written.

The second thing that distinguished Campbell is the fact that he became a preacher of international fame and acclaimed far and wide by enemies as well as friends. Many of his foes thought he was the greatest preacher they had ever heard, whether they agreed with him or not. His friends almost deified him because of his unsurpassed skill at preaching.

In the third place, Campbell became an accomplished debater, outshining all others of the time. Though he resisted debates to begin with, after his debate with John Walker at Mt. Pleasant, Ohio in 1820, he decided the debate was an effective method of advancing the Restoration cause. He became a noted and enthusiastic debater.

Campbell rode horseback all the way from Bethany down to Washington, Mason County, Kentucky in 1823, to debate W.L. McCalla. McCalla, a Presbyterian preacher at Augusta, challenged Campbell to a debate after his debate with Walker. Following his debate with McCalla, Robert Owen challenged him to a debate. Now Robert Owen was one of the most noted socialists in America at the time. He was an English industrialist, but he adopted socialism and infidelity when he came to America. He established the New Harmony Community in Indiana, a part of which has been restored. Owen had pronounced his Manifesto throughout the land, claiming that if everyone accepted what it taught, it would eliminate the Bibles from all printing presses. Incensed by such presumption, Campbell decided to take Owen on in a debate at Cincinnati, Ohio in 1839.

It is said that Owen visited Campbell at his home in Bethany as they were preparing for the debate. Campbell was a successful farmer, and he took Owen out on his farm to show him his cattle. As they were talking, Owen remarked to Campbell, "Do you see that cow?" Campbell waited as Owen continued: "I'm just like that cow. The cow has no fear of death; it fills itself with grass by day and rests by night without a worry in the world, and with no fear of the end of its life upon this earth."

It then was Campbell's turn. "Yes, sir," he said to Owen, "that cow is just like you as you described. It has no fear of death at all, but let me tell you, Mr. Owen, the cow does not have any hope either. The cow is just like you, with no fear and with no hope either. You do not have a fear, but neither do you have a hope."

Campbell attacked a variety of errors in the debates in which he engaged. He and Owen built their debate around the concept of socialistic fidelity in contrast with fidelity to the gospel of Jesus Christ. Campbell held his fourth debate with Bishop John Purcell in Cincinnati. They debated the tenets of Catholicism, the apostasy of the church of Christ, and the Reformation Movement. His final debate was held in 1843, with Nathan L. Rice, a Presbyterian preacher in Lexington, Kentucky. Campbell's debate with John Walker and the one with W. L. McCalla had placed him in good standing with the Baptists because he defended immersion and opposed infant baptism. After his debate with Robert Owen, he became the fair-haired boy in all Christendom, a hero to all those who accepted Christianity. He represented Protestantism against the encroachment of a totalitarian state of Catholicism and stressed other points in his debate with John Purcell. When he debated Owen, though, he came to represent Christianity against paganism, infidelity, and socialism. Comparatively speaking, the N.L. Rice debate was somewhat anti-climactic. Rice showed some of the inconsistencies of Campbell's arguments, particularly as set forth in the Lunenburg letter which Campbell had written to a woman in Virginia about the state of sectarians.

The fourth role by which Campbell distinguished himself was as an educator. Even before coming to America, he had had some experience in education. His father had organized a seminary in Ireland and when Thomas left to come to America in 1807, Alexander took over the academy and ran it for a year before leaving for America to join his father. Education really put Campbell in contact with a type of people who might understand better what he was advocating. In 1818 he organized the Buffalo Seminary, which met in his mansion. It met on the upper floor and his family moved to the basement to live while the seminary was in session. Some speculate that living in a damp unvented basement was part of the cause for his wife and several daughters dying of tuberculosis.

After the seminary was closed, Campbell turned his attention to founding Bethany College, which was established in Bethany, West

Virginia in 1840, and which continues to be an outstanding monument to him as an educator and scholar. Campbell was rightfully accepted into educational circles as a man of great renown. As a writer, debater, educator, and preacher, Alexander Campbell ranks with the most successful statesmen of his day.

Alexander Campbell's determination to be remembered as a leading champion of the Restoration Movement was bolstered by the widespread and unquestioned display of his multiple talents. He was, indeed, a strong educator who won renown and acceptance into prestigious educational circles. His skills as writer and debater won respect even from those who were stung. And his preaching and efforts to restore the New Testament Church left indelible marks. The difference which Campbell made in the inception and spread of the Restoration Movement can never be measured in time for it is still woven into the fabric of our lives. We must await eternity to observe the contribution which Alexander Campbell made in the early efforts to restore New Testament Christianity and the ancient order of things. But God be thanked that his influence is among us in calling us back to the Bible.

CHAPTER SIX

THE CHRISTIAN SCHOLAR—BIOGRAPHY OF HALL LAURIE CALHOUN

Hall Laurie Calhoun was a fascinating person and an extremely private individual in all respects, highly complex in all that he did, thought, or said. He touched every base in the Restoration Movement during a long and prestigious career. Along the way he became identified with every group that emerged as he was weaving his way in and out of the spiritual and intellectual events. His complexity, brilliance, and outstanding achievements are set forth and substantiated in the biographical study *The Christian Scholar*. The authors, Adron Doran (author of this present book) and Julian Earnest Choate, devoted four years to the challenging task of collecting and evaluating material, putting it together, and persuading the Gospel Advocate Company to publish it.

The name Hall Laurie was given a new son by his parents, John Shelton Calhoun and Louisa Hall Calhoun. Hall was the maiden name of his mother, while Laurie honored the physician who attended his mother at his birth. So it was that Hall Laurie Calhoun entered the world and began what was destined to be a very productive and influential life.

Calhoun was truly the protege, as we claim, of John William McGarvey. McGarvey probably had a greater influence upon him than all other associates combined. The definitive biography was so entitled because Hall Laurie Calhoun was indeed a scholar; his scholarship remains, as it was from his early years, unquestioned.

I became deeply interested in the role which this man played after moving to Lexington, Kentucky in 1977, the place where most of the literature of the period originated among the writers who lived there and involved themselves in the Restoration Movement. Within easy access were the libraries at the University of Kentucky, Transylvania University, the Lexington Theological Seminary, and the Lexington Public Library. All are rich with holdings concerning the Restoration Movement and the individuals involved with it. Now, my interest in Calhoun evolved from a prior concern with the life and works of John William McGarvey. I felt strongly that McGarvey had never been presented in the light and with the depth which his stature merited. The real McGarvey was still an enigma, still unknown to the brotherhood to a great degree and therefore unappreciated.

I came upon more than I anticipated. That McGarvey was a great scholar was patently known. He was also an outstanding preacher and teacher of the first order. But something else was interesting, even tantalizing; here and there were persistent little mentions of Hall Laurie Calhoun. Some comments were complimentary; other statements were less than kind. I sensed a growing desire to know more, to put together a whole picture where only snippets and fragments existed.

The memory of an earlier meeting with Calhoun added spice to the study for me. In 1929, when I was a second-quarter sophomore at Freed-Hardeman College, the church at Puryear, Tennessee, invited me to lead the singing for a revival meeting in which Calhoun would do the preaching. The older man impressed me as a most excellent Bible scholar and as one of the most tremendous preachers and pulpit orators I had ever heard. I learned during the week of the meeting that Calhoun held a Ph.D. degree from Harvard University. Never had I seen or heard anyone with a Ph.D. degree, much less from the Divinity School at Harvard University. This was in the time when most elementary and high school teachers did not even have college degrees, and in 1929 not one member of the faculty at Freed-Hardeman College had a doctor's degree. Many of them had earned Masters Degrees. So Calhoun's achievement in academics was fascinating and even awe-inspiring.

One day as I recall, I mustered enough courage to ask Calhoun about the subject on which he had written his doctoral dissertation. "Why, son," was the reply, "if I told you, you would not understand."

Interest—and perhaps the sting—lingered throughout the years. There came a day when scholar Choate and I contacted Harvard University where Calhoun's dissertation remains on file in the library, and learned that the subject was, "The Remains of the Old Latin Translation of Leviticus." Calhoun had taken Jerome's Vulgate of the Book of Leviticus which had been translated into Latin, reversed the translation, and written a critique of the Latin translation.

I could not have done what Calhoun did, but I still think he should have dealt a little more gently with me in talking about it.

The voice of Calhoun entered households and business places spread over a wide area in Middle Tennessee through broadcasts over the Nashville radio station WLAC. From the auditorium of the Central Church of Christ in Nashville he could be heard preaching during the last ten years of his life, and became a familiar preacher throughout the region. It is said that a radio in every business place in each town would be tuned to WLAC at noon each day and a person could walk down the street, going from store to store, without missing a sentence that Calhoun uttered.

I was among the listeners, then living in Graves County of Western Kentucky. A trip in 1933 to Chattanooga brought me through Nashville and made it possible to stop at the Central Church to hear Calhoun's noon sermon. My brother Basil, W.W. Heflin, Truman Carney, and I were on our way to attend the Foy Wallace-Charles Neal debate. After the sermon that day we enjoyed a pleasant conversation together with no mention of his dissertation subject!

The connection with Calhoun grew in subtle and unexpected ways. The director of the lectureships at Freed-Hardeman University asked me to prepare a lecture for the 1980 lectureship, presenting the research I had done on Hall Calhoun. After accepting the invitation, I wrote a letter to Dr. Choate who was teaching at David Lipscomb University at the time, and requested that he get some of his advanced students to do some research in the university library, the library of the Disciples Historical Society, and the *Gospel Advocate* files. He kindly consented to do so, but not much time elapsed before he decided that he did not want these senior students to do the study; he wanted to do the research in Nashville on Calhoun himself. So Dr. Choate proposed that we set out on a collaborative effort which would result in a complete biography of Calhoun. He himself was finding bits, pieces, and parcels of Calhoun's life and works in Nashville as I was doing in Lexington. Together we were to be able to present Hall Laurie Calhoun in a full and true perspective. An agreement was reached and work on the project was underway.

Reports which we found were sometimes contradictory and confusing. When Calhoun left the Christian church in 1925, the liberals literally vilified him. They dropped him "like a hot potato." They had nothing to do with him and had few complimentary words to say about him in their writings. But on the other hand, most of the churches of Christ almost deified him. To them he had done no wrong. He had known no evil. He had heard no evil. He had spoken no evil. However, some members of the churches of Christ were quite skeptical of his sincerity in leaving the Christian church. Who was he, really? It soon became all too obvious that the task of the biographers—a challenging one—would be to determine who Calhoun actually was and to present him in his true light. Could this be done, when he was not even known very well by his own family? His children did not know him very well. His grandsons do not know him at all. Thus, the task of ferreting out from opposing opinions and favorable opinions would be difficult indeed, but we were on our way.

Hall Laurie Calhoun was born in Conyersville on December 11, 1863, and reared in that rural agricultural community of civil district number fourteen in Henry County, Tennessee. He received his first training in the Conyersville Male/Female Academy. He attended school there until about the sixth or seventh grade. His parents transferred him in 1877 to Mayfield, Kentucky, and enrolled him in the Mayfield Seminary, which seems to have been a middle school or a junior high school. Calhoun's brother-in-law, W.T. Shelton, whom his sister Mattie had married, was preaching for a Restored Church in Mayfield at the time. Hall Laurie spent two years in Mayfield, from 1877 to 1879. Then when the Sheltons moved to Union City, Tennessee where W.T. Shelton was to preach for the Christian Church, Calhoun went with them to enroll in the high school in that city. He stayed in Union City for four years, graduating from high school in 1883. He remained for two more years to teach in the high school from which he had just graduated.

Calhoun returned to Conyersville to prepare for his examination to enter the West Point Military Academy. He was required to pass a technical examination, so he spent two years preparing himself, especially in the area of science and mathematics while teaching in the academy.

The day came when Hall was to leave home for New York, where he would report to West Point, the first step toward a military career. His father finally told him that he did not want his son to go into the military. He and his wife hated the very thought of their son becoming a professional soldier. They asked him to give up the idea of making a career of the Army and told him they would somehow get the money necessary to send him to college.

Hall perhaps knew himself less well than his family did. They knew that he, as well as they, had always wanted to preach. His father made arrangements for him to go to the College of the Bible in Lexington, Kentucky, where he could sit at the feet of John William McGarvey and others of the Restoration Movement.

There was rejoicing in the Calhoun household. Hall enrolled in the College of the Bible, which was a part of Kentucky University, in 1888. Kentucky University was the successor to old Bacon College, which was founded in Georgetown, Kentucky in 1836, with Walter Scott as the first president. Bacon College had moved later to Harrodsburg, and then in 1865 it moved to Lexington and merged with Transylvania University, which had been dormant for a number of years. The College of the Bible was organized by McGarvey as one of the colleges of Kentucky University. Calhoun earned a Baccalaureate Degree from Kentucky University and a classical diploma from the College of the Bible in 1892. After graduating, he was requested by the university to remain for two years and teach in the preparatory school. When those two years had passed, he returned with his wife and a baby girl to Conyersville, where he planned to take care of his aging parents.

But other circumstances and other opportunities were to change Calhoun's plans. In 1887, Georgia Robertson Christian College was built in Henderson, Tennessee. J.H. Robertson, who was a wealthy farmer in West Tennessee, agreed to contribute $5,000 if the Tennessee Christian Missionary Society would raise another $5,000 to erect a building and name the college after his daughter who had died some time before. The project was completed and Calhoun was invited to deliver the address when the building was dedicated. Calhoun became acquainted with A.G. Freed, N.B. Hardeman, L.L. Brigance, and others connected with the college. He had already become acquainted with E.C. McDougle during a meeting which he had conducted in Huntingdon, Tennessee, where McDougle preached. Calhoun had preached in Paducah, Kentucky and Franklin, Tennessee, as well as conducting gospel meetings. At the beginning of the 1900 school year, Calhoun went to Henderson to teach in the Georgia Robertson Christian College over which Freed and McDougle were presiding as co-presidents. The college at that time was under the control of the State Missionary Society, and the Henderson church used an organ in worship where the faculty were members.

Meanwhile, McGarvey seemed to be lying in wait and observing the progress which Calhoun was making. So in 1901, McGarvey invited Calhoun to return to the College of the Bible as a member of the faculty. He received McGarvey's letter of invitation with great joy. The letter from McGarvey to Calhoun has been lost, but the reply from Calhoun still exists. Yes, he was highly elated at the prospect of teaching in the College of the Bible! However, McGarvey insisted that Calhoun advance his academic preparation by earning advanced degrees from some prestigious university. Calhoun chose the Yale Divinity School and laid plans to enroll. Once arrangements were completed, he took his family and struck out to New Haven, Connecticut. The College of the Bible arranged for him to draw $50.00 a month while he was attending graduate school with the understanding that he would return to the College of the Bible when his studies were completed.

Calhoun spent one year at Yale University and met the requirements for a Bachelor of Divinity Degree. The Lexington Theological Seminary requires a person to take three years to earn a Baccalaureate of Divinity Degree today. It was rather amazing that Calhoun earned his B.D. Degree in one year! But after a year at Yale, he decided that he had learned about all that institution had to offer him. He had mastered all that they would teach him. So he laid his plans to go to Harvard. The Dean of the Harvard School of Divinity discouraged the transfer, but he was so set on going to Harvard that he refused to be deterred. Unwillingly, the dean admitted him to the divinity school. In two more years he had earned a Master of Arts Degree and a Doctor of Philosophy Degree. By this point in time he had earned a Bachelor of Arts Degree from Kentucky University, a Bachelor of Divinity Degree from Yale, and both a Master of Arts Degree and a Ph.D.

Degree from Harvard. These achievements are the basis for our declaring him to be a Christian scholar.

Following these three years of advanced study at Yale and Harvard, he returned in 1904 to Lexington to join the faculty of the College of the Bible. Calhoun was received with open arms amid glowing reports that this young scholar of the Restoration Movement was destined for great things. He served as a professor in the Bible College and as minister for the Nicholasville society-organ Christian Church. Later he was appointed Dean of the College of the Bible after W.C. Morro resigned in the spring of 1911. McGarvey died on October 13, 1911, and Calhoun was selected by the curators as acting president. It must be concluded at this point that Hall Laurie Calhoun had become one of the most outstanding scholars in the brotherhood, with bright promise of becoming one of the most distinguished preachers.

What were the forces that went into shaping the career of this extraordinary young man? And, more significantly, what early religious experiences bent this twig? His achievements inspire many other questions. Calhoun was born in a little community in Henry County, Tennessee. His ancestors had traveled from North Carolina and settled in Tennessee. In 1848, his parents came from North Carolina to Henry County by way of Wilson and Davidson Counties.

When Hall Laurie was twelve years old he attended a revival at the little Methodist Church in his home community—it being the only religious institution there. His father had arranged the farm work so that the boy would be free to attend the day and night services. He went to the revival intent upon "getting religion." He joined his peers at the mourner's bench at each service. The church members admonished him, prayed over him, and sang over him, but he recalled later that he never could detect a feeling different from the one he had before he went to the mourner's bench on the first night. All around him his peers were declaring triumphantly that they had "prayed through." But not he! He could not detect a changed feeling within himself. At last he decided that he must have had an experience he was seeking without being able to recognize it for what it was. So he announced to the eager audience that he had "gotten religion." Yet, what he took away with him was a gnawing, persisting dissatisfaction. He confessed his doubts to his mother and his older sister, Mary. They tried to assure him that he should not worry for his doubts were normal in people who had just been saved. Everyone promised that his fears and anxieties would soon pass and he would experience the joy and comfort of salvation.

Calhoun labored under a blanket of uneasiness for some two years, at which time he went to Mayfield to attend the seminary. A gospel meeting was in progress at the Mayfield Christian Church, and Calhoun attended this protracted meeting for forty-two nights. After listening to and pondering over the gospel sermons which he heard, he accepted the invitation, confessed his faith in Jesus Christ, repented of his sins, and was buried with the Lord by baptism into death for the remission of his sins. The name of the one who baptized him is not known. However, writing about his conversion sixty years later, Calhoun said that he had never once doubted or regretted that he had been baptized for the remission of his sins, for he could find examples of conversion in the Bible just like his. Prior to the time that Calhoun had gone to Mayfield, W.T. Shelton, his brother-in-law, had conducted a gospel meeting in the Methodist meeting house in Conyersville. On the first night of the meeting, Martha Louisa Calhoun went forward and made the good confession and was baptized by Shelton. Calhoun's father was later baptized as was his sister, shaking the very foundation of Calhoun's religious convictions at the time. He did not think that such would ever happen to him. He had protested that the Campbellites would never get him.

Now when Calhoun graduated from the College of the Bible in 1892, he returned to Conyersville to teach and to preach. He was pretty well set to teach school and to preach among his brethren in West Tennessee and West Kentucky. Soon he was in great demand as a preacher. He went to the Tenth Street Christian Church in Paducah, Kentucky to preach in a meeting. At the close of the revival the church asked him to become the regular, full-time preacher. Though he continued to live in Conyersville, he and his wife commuted by train from Conyersville to Paducah. This arrangement was maintained for a year.

The church in Paducah at the time was affiliated with the missionary society, and it had introduced an organ into worship. So it was known as a society-organ Christian Church. During this period of time, some of the churches of the Restoration were called organ-society churches, and others were called non-organ and non-society churches. The introduction of the organ into the worship of the Paducah church was due to the influence of J.H. Bondurant. He was a wealthy storekeeper who furnished the money to construct a building and then exercised his prerogative to purchase and install an organ simply because he happened to like instrumental music in the worship. Now Calhoun was opposed to instrumental music in worship, as was McGarvey. But Calhoun did not speak out against it. Someone asked him why he did not throw his influence into the controversy and stop the use of the organ. He replied that he feared his opposition would divide the church; he did not want to be guilty of division, so he remained silent. He thought that it was better to use the organ in worship than to divide the church. From such a brilliant man, that seems to be rather faulty and elementary reasoning. Yet, sadly enough, there are brethren in 1997 among churches of Christ who take the same position which Calhoun took. A hundred years have not removed all the faulty thinking! It would be more accurate to conclude that the people who introduced the organ divided the church, rather than those who opposed its introduction.

After remaining in Paducah for a year, Calhoun moved to Franklin, Tennessee, south of Nashville, and began to preach for a non-organ and non-society church of Christ. Calhoun decided that he could play the organ and sing or just sing without the organ. He could be for the organ some and against it a little, whichever way the brethren preferred. Calhoun, in this respect, is like a young school teacher who applied to the local trustee of a public school for a job. The trustee asked the young teacher whether he taught that the world was round or square. "Well, sir," the eager young man replied, "I'm prepared to teach it either way." Calhoun was like that with respect to the organ. So he stayed on in Franklin until 1900, when he moved to Henderson and taught in the Georgia Robertson Christian College.

Excitement, with increasing momentum, accompanied Calhoun into the arenas of religious conflict, no matter how sincerely he feared the dividing of the church. One can imagine that a person with Calhoun's traits and talents would find himself in deep and intense conflict over issues and ideas, as well as over his own likes and dislikes, and his personal clashes with individuals. Edward Ormond Hale wrote a thesis to meet the requirements for a Bachelor of Divinity Degree at the Lexington Theological Seminary in 1978 on the topic, "A Man in Controversy: Hall Laurie Calhoun." Actually though, it did not seem to us that Calhoun was so much a man of controversy as he was a man in conflict. He never seemed to create a controversy as much as he found himself in conflict over controversies. He may be more accurately described in the light of his conflicts rather than at the center of controversy. The apostle Paul engaged in a great controversy on Mars Hill (Acts 17:22-31), but it was not that kind of situation in which Calhoun often found himself. So evident were his conflicts that William Clayton Bower, a latter-day dean at the College of the Bible, in an interview with me, said that Calhoun had a "split personality."

Bower diagnosed Calhoun as a schizophrenic. He said that the reason that Calhoun suffered from schizophrenia and a split personality was that he was caught in a bind between the conservative view of the churches of Christ in Tennessee and the liberalism to which he was exposed in Yale and Harvard. To know the man reveals him to staunchly repudiate that diagnosis! The record does not show him to be a schizophrenic. Such an assertion by Bower suggests an effort on Bower's part to play down the controversy in the College of the Bible in 1917. There are letters that Calhoun wrote to McGarvey during the very time that he was "under the influences" of the liberals in Yale and Harvard. Calhoun told McGarvey that he found great difference between what McGarvey had taught him and what he was being exposed to in the eastern divinity schools. He wrote that he was learning what the liberals were teaching him only because he wanted to meet the requirements for the academic degrees which he was seeking. Calhoun wrote to McGarvey that the more he was exposed to liberalism in the classes at Yale and Harvard, the more precious the "grand old gospel" was to him. He declared that the Bible meant more to him than it ever had before. Why, he gave absolutely no evidence at all of being a split personality. He knew the Bible, and he knew where he stood with regard to the teachings of the Bible, regardless of contradictory views of destructive criticism. Now, William Clayton Bower was an educational sociologist, not a Bible scholar, and one can understand the basis of his indictment. Associates who knew Bower recall that his stand on religion was weak, his knowledge and practice insubstantial—making him less than a credible evaluator of Hall Laurie Calhoun. I interviewed Bower when he was 90 years old and attended his funeral when he died at 92.

It should be remembered that Calhoun had not been exposed to the operations of the Missionary Society or to the use of instrumental music in worship until he moved to Lexington in 1888 at the age of twenty-five. He had been baptized in Western Kentucky. His parents had been baptized in West Tennessee and held membership in the old Blood River Church of Christ. Then later, James A. Harding went to Conyersville and established a congregation of the church of Christ. Obviously, Hall Laurie had been influenced by the conservatism of the church up to the time he went to Lexington. During the year that he arrived in Lexington, the Main Street Church introduced an organ into the worship. When the organ made its appearance in the Main Street building, there was so much opposition to its use that the elders bought a little cottage organ and hid it behind a curtain on the stage so that no one could see it while it was being played. They were not offended in hearing the instrument, but the elders thought that if it could not be seen, there would be less objection and less chance that the church would divide.

McGarvey spoke out against what the Main Street congregation had done. Calhoun went to the Broadway Christian Church which McGarvey had established in 1870. It was at the Broadway Church while teaching a Bible class, that he met Mary Etta Stacy, who, he recalled, came down the aisle to join the class. This girl impressed him so much that he said to himself then and there, "I am going to marry that girl." He began straightway to woo her and soon pressed his suit to marriage. She accepted his proposal and they were married in Paris, Tennessee.

The following years were characterized by conflicts. Calhoun continued to worship at Broadway while attending school in Lexington, and McGarvey remained there as an elder until 1903. When the Broadway Church introduced an instrument of music into the worship, McGarvey and others left and went to the Chestnut Street Christian Church, which did not use instrumental music in its worship. During the final years that Calhoun was teaching at the College of the Bible, he preached for the old Providence Christian Church, which had been established in 1817. The Providence Church is located about halfway between Lexington and Nicholasville, right on the Fayette County line in Jessamine County. The congregation was established by Jacob Creath, Sr., as a Baptist church. When John Allen Gano converted Creath to the truth, the name was changed from a Baptist church to a restored New Testament church. Calhoun was preaching there in 1910 when the women of the congregation got up a petition to introduce an organ into the worship at Providence. They circulated the document throughout the community and many endorsed it.

Years later, a ninety-two year-old woman recalled to me the time of the organ's introduction at Providence and shared the details with me. She was the daughter of an elder of the Providence Church at the time the organ was introduced. Alma Browning remembered the incident well. I asked her if she remembered when the organ was put in. "Why, young man," she answered, "I reckon I do. I played it!" She was thirteen years old at the time. Her mother, who was a Baptist, signed the petition. Asked about Hall Calhoun's response, she said that she did not remember a thing in the world about any opposition on his part to the organ being brought into the Providence Church. However, Mrs. Browning did go on to recall that one elder, Mr. Marrs, who was supposed to wait on the Lord's table on the Sunday morning that the organ was introduced, refused to do so. Instead, he took the opportunity to express his disapproval of the organ. Then he walked out of the meeting house and went to the Chestnut Street Christian Church in Lexington—the congregation where McGarvey had gone. This occurrence at the Providence Church is typical of the many instances of conflict in which Calhoun was involved.

While Calhoun was preaching in Paducah, Kentucky and in Franklin, Tennessee, during a period from 1896 to 1900, James A. Harding and David Lipscomb invited him to come to Nashville and be interviewed for a position on the faculty of the old Nashville Bible School. He was very eager to teach there so he went for the interview. The two men talked with him over a period of four days, and finally Lipscomb and Harding told him that they would give him a teaching job and arrange for a preaching assignment at Fayetteville, Tennessee. They proposed to Calhoun that he reside in Nashville and commute to Fayetteville to preach, but they would require of him that he renounce his affiliation with the Christian Church and his fellowship with John William McGarvey. He immediately and firmly replied that he would do no such thing. He considered McGarvey to be as good a Christian as either of them. Displaying more than a little righteous indignation, he turned to Lipscomb and retorted, "Why, Mr. Lipscomb, you preach among organ churches just like I preach among organ churches." "I know I do," Mr. Lipscomb admitted, "but you stay too long."

Well, who can say how long a fellow would have to stay at a place before being tainted by corrupt practices? At any rate, Lipscomb and Harding were firm; they would give Calhoun a job only under these stated conditions. Calhoun was at least equally firm, so he refused the offer.

In 1900, Calhoun went to Georgia Robertson Christian College in Henderson, Tennessee where he taught for a year. When Calhoun arrived at Georgia Robertson College, he found the institution to be affiliated with the Tennessee Missionary Society. Furthermore, the church in Henderson used an organ in the worship services. At that time, A.G. Freed, E.C. McDougle, N.B. Hardeman, and L.L. Brigance were all members of the faculty at the Georgia Robertson Christian College. They were also members of an organ-church and were teaching in a college affiliated with the missionary society!

Calhoun felt perfectly at home in this familiar situation. With the decisions which he had made, he was ready to go to Lexington to teach in the College of the Bible. This was the point at which he crossed his "Rubicon." He had now cast his lot with the Christian Church with McGarvey and with the College of the Bible. Calhoun's year-long experience in Henderson seasoned him well for his new assignment in Lexington. He preached for the non-organ Christian Church in Newbern, Tennessee.

Only a few decades later, few would remember that Freed-Hardeman University had evolved from little Georgia Robertson Christian College, an affiliate of the missionary society, nor would many connect it with the organ that was used in the Christian Church where Freed and Hardeman worshiped. Freed and Hardeman later left the college and the Christian Church and established the Henderson Church of Christ and the National Teachers College.

It is amazing how rapidly Calhoun did rise in the affairs of the Christian Church in only a few short years. It should be remembered that John William McGarvey was a "man of the Book," as Dean W.C. Morro characterized him. However, McGarvey never did identify with the church of Christ as James A. Harding had done in Winchester, Kentucky in 1887. McGarvey was always identified with the Christian Church, but he refused to hold membership in a congregation where an organ was used. Yet, he would preach for a congregation without regard to the presence or absence of the organ.

During the year 1917, one of the greatest controversies within the Restoration Movement took place within the academic community of the College of the Bible. Calhoun found himself in conflict with President R.H. Crossfield, four liberal faculty members, as well as with the Board of Trustees over the teaching of evolution and destructive criticism in the classrooms. McGarvey had literally groomed Calhoun to succeed him as president of the College of the Bible. Just as Elijah had placed his mantle upon Elisha as his successor, so McGarvey worked at preparing and training Calhoun to take over when he would leave. McGarvey died in the fall of 1911, and Calhoun was left to "paddle his own canoe." W.C. Morro had come to the College of the Bible as Professor of Greek and Christian Doctrine in 1906, and later was promoted to the deanship. He resigned in early 1911 to take a position at Butler University, and thus the deanship was left open. McGarvey recommended Calhoun to succeed Morro and the Board of Trustees elected him. After McGarvey's death, however, Calhoun was named acting president of the College of the Bible. He surely felt some trepidation, for he had only to look about him to realize that he was literally standing alone against strong ideological and religious opponents.

The list was long. R.H. Crossfield, one of the most liberal minded preachers within the ranks of the Christian Church, had come to Transylvania University as president in 1908. McGarvey died and Isaiah Boone Grubbs retired. Robert Graham and Moses Easterly Lard had also died. Professor Jefferson had fallen on the way to school, victim of a heart attack. With these conservative faithfuls gone to their rewards, and the roster of opponents so overwhelmingly liberal, the situation looked dark for the sole representative of the "old guard" in the College of the Bible. Calhoun was the only one left who still taught what McGarvey had taught and who used McGarvey's approach to teaching.

At this point in time, Crossfield instigated proceedings that finally led to his becoming president of both Transylvania University and the College of the Bible. He announced to the Trustees that he was going to leave the presidency of Transylvania University and go back to a Christian Church pulpit. But he advised the Board of Trustees that it ought to select a man to be president of both Transylvania University and the College of the Bible. The Board thought the suggestion a wise one. The Board believed that such a move could reduce conflicts that had long existed within each institution and between the university and the college. McGarvey and Regent John Bowman had engaged in serious controversies for years, and even Calhoun and Crossfield had earlier crossed swords.

However, the move made by the Board was surprising to many in both institutions. Crossfield was asked to remain in Lexington and the joint Boards met in 1912 to elect Crossfield as president of both Transylvania University and the College of the Bible. His election gave Crossfield the green light to proceed in the liberal direction that he had wanted to go. He immediately set about filling four vacancies on the faculty of the College of the Bible with men of his own convictions. Crossfield first named Alonzo Willard Fortune and William Clayton Bower. Next he appointed George W. Hembree and Elmer Snoddy to the faculty. Hembree managed never to raise his voice or bat an eye about any conflict in the college, seemingly either unaware or unconcerned. Elmer E. Snoddy, a brother-in-law of Bower, was one of the most radical and outspoken among the new teachers. He was an outstanding scholar and an excellent teacher, but he expressed the same views which his brother-in-law held.

What happened at the College of the Bible in 1917 is treated in the Calhoun biography under the chapter heading "A Firestorm in the Bluegrass." And the conflagration was a firestorm indeed! The fire was not confined only to the Bluegrass, but it swept throughout the brotherhood and among individuals at home and abroad. On March 12, 1917, Benjamin Franklin Battenfield and a group of mature Bible students in the College of the Bible wrote and mailed letters to three hundred Christian preachers asking them to use their influence to protect the college against the new theology, destructive criticism, and evolution which was being taught in the classrooms. These letters aroused all types of dissension and all kinds of opposition to the college. Many brethren who had previously supported the college were greatly disturbed. The basis of the students' contention was that the teachers were all destructive critics, that Bower was teaching that Jehovah was no more than the tribal God of Israel, and that the *Pithecanthropus Erectus* (Java Man), was the missing link between man and lower animals. Snoddy was labeled a "hard evolutionist" who considered the first chapter of Genesis to be no more than poetry.

Complicated as this conflict was and heated as the controversy became, it was the teaching of evolution which became the main thrust of the indictments against the four faculty members. It is significant that the materials about the conflict are filed under the subject of "evolution" in the Transylvania University library.

Similar indictments were brought against Fortune. According to students, Fortune taught that the writings which comprise the New Testament are inspired, but the men who wrote them were not. It is hard to comprehend how the writings of the apostles were inspired when they themselves were not. Fortune said that he was a theistic evolutionist. He also denied the resurrection of the physical body of Christ and the plenary inspiration of the Bible. Strange teachings to be aired within the halls of the College of the Bible!

Crossfield soon mounted a counter-offensive to defuse the effect of his accusers. The Board read the charges and the counter charges, and finally decided to conduct a formal hearing. The curators were called together, and on May 1, 1917, the first meeting was held for the purpose of investigating the charges that Battenfield and others had filed. There were fifteen sessions, and right in the middle of the hearings Bower charged the curators with conducting a "heresy trial." Bower contended that he was no heretic and that he would have no part in a heresy trial. Nevertheless, the hearings proceeded during which Calhoun and some of the students appeared as witnesses. Following the conclusion of the sessions, the Board wrote what surely must be one of the most biased documents that any group of intelligent men could write regarding such an important and critical issue. They had structured the hearing; they had intimidated the witnesses; they and threatened students in every way they could conceive. The report which was written was nothing more than a whitewash. The hearings had been completed and the faculty and the President had been exonerated and found not guilty as charged. It was declared by the trustees that the faculty had been teaching in the traditions of the Restoration Movement and the Christian Church and had not deviated one whit. The Chairman of the Board was Mark Collis, who was the minister of the Broadway Christian Church at the time. Collis voted in favor of exonerating the faculty, but with strong reservations. He said he voted for the report, but reserved the right to oppose it later. The Board did not give Collis an opportunity to change his mind; at the next meeting they voted him out of the chairmanship after twenty-five years of service to the College of the Bible. A chairman with more liberal leanings was elected Chairman.

McAlester and Tucker say in their *Journeys Through Faith* that the liberals won the battle of the Book at the College of the Bible in 1917. The college went with the liberal element of the Christian Church and ousted the conservative element. *The Christian Standard* took up the cause of Calhoun and his conservative group. *The Christian Standard* and the *Christian Evangelist* fought the war for a number of months. Ralph Records, Chairman of the Department of Chemistry at Transylvania University, resigned because he was convinced by the hearings that the Board of Trustees agreed with destructive criticism and evolutionary ideas which were being taught in the College of the Bible. Records then continued his teaching career at Bethany College. He later was associated with the Cincinnati Seminary.

Calhoun often quoted McGarvey and Grubbs about their feelings toward the College of the Bible as well as stating his own reactions to all that had transpired. Calhoun quoted Grubbs and McGarvey as having said that they would rather see the College of the Bible sink to the bottom of the ocean than to watch it evolve into a place where destructive criticism and evolution were taught. Calhoun said that it was with a heavy heart that he severed his associations with a college which had meant more to him than life itself. However, circumstances dictated a painful decision; he resigned, and from 1917 until 1925 he taught at Bethany College.

When Calhoun arrived at Bethany, President Thomas E. Cramblett was in the midst of a discussion about destructive criticism and liberalism, two devilish elements which were creeping into many institutions of higher education. Cramblett declared that as long as he lived and served as president of Bethany College, he would have nothing to do with the new theology. But tragedy struck in 1919, when Cramblett took blood poisoning and suddenly died. The Board of Trustees elected as his replacement Claude Goodnight, a product of the Divinity School at the University of Chicago. While there he had become identified with the Campbell Institute. It was not far into this new administration before Calhoun began to see signs of Bethany College being moved in the same direction that the College of the Bible had gone. Furthermore, the Christian Church in Bethany was moving in the same direction that the Central Christian Church in Lexington had taken, the victim of aggressive, liberal theology. Calhoun realized at last that it was time to make some drastic and life-changing decisions. He would renounce his affiliation with the Christian Church; he would resign his position on the faculty at Bethany College; and he would return to his native land in Tennessee. He soon followed through with all three decisions, thus he was in a position in 1925 to become co-President with N.B. Hardeman at Freed-Hardeman College. During the time in which he served as co-President, he also filled the position of full-time minister of the Henderson Church of Christ. It is not surprising that Calhoun received serious opposition from his former brethren in the Christian Church. As a result of this criticism, he finally decided to write an article for *The Gospel Advocate* which he titled "Why I Did It." The article explained to his critics that he had simply changed his mind regarding the practices of the Christian Church. He had simply ceased to believe in the practices and beliefs which he had been defending. One of the reasons that he changed his mind was that the American Christian Missionary Society seemed to be robbing the local churches of their autonomy, and he feared that the church would eventually be weakened. He also said that he believed instrumental music was corrupting the worship of the New Testament Church, while the teachings of evolution and destructive criticism were destroying Christianity.

Calhoun's work in Henderson was all too brief, lasting but one year. He left Henderson and moved to Nashville in 1926. Soon afterward, he suffered a severe nervous breakdown. But with proper care from his family and friends, he recovered during the summer and was able to begin preaching for the Belmont Church of Christ in Nashville. After a short tenure at Belmont, he moved to the Central Church of Christ and became the radio preacher for that great congregation. During this time, he also taught classes at David Lipscomb College.

The conflict which took place in the College of the Bible in 1917 continued to have far-reaching effects. One result was a division within the Christian Church between the conservatives, who called themselves the Independent Christian Church, and the liberals, who labeled themselves the Christian Church (Disciples of Christ). It should be remembered that when the Christian Church introduced the organ and affiliated with the American Christian Missionary Society, it became a separate and distinct denomination. There was so much difference between the organ and society people and the non-organ and non-society people, that in 1906 the Federal Bureau of the Census listed the Christian Church and the Church of Christ separately. David Lipscomb and J.W. Shepherd helped Director North see the differences and influenced him to enter the Christian Church under a separate listing. In 1927, the conservative element of the Christian Church withdrew from the liberal element and formed the North American Convention. In 1968, the International Convention of the Disciples of Christ created what they called the Provisional Design, which formed the Disciples of Christ as a full-fledged denomination in word and deed. In later years the Disciples of Christ have voted to form an "ecumenical partnership" with the United Churches of Christ. One of the problems we face in dealing with historians of the Disciples of Christ is that they are bent on rewriting the history of the Restoration Movement. They are trying to move the Disciples of Christ farther back in time than they can be rightfully identified. Anthony Dunivant, for example, is a historian at the Lexington Theological Seminary. Dr. Dunivant recently wrote a history of the Central Christian Church at Lexington and took the Disciples back through the Main Street Church to the Hill Street Church. But the Disciples of Christ were not at Hill Street. The Christians were at Hill Street, a congregation established by Barton Stone in 1816. Yet another historian, Lester G. McAllister, wrote a biography of Z.T. Sweeney in 1968 in which he said Sweeney (1849-1926) was identified with the Disciples of Christ. Now it is misleading when deliberate anachronisms are foisted on readers trying to seek out the truth regarding the history of the Restoration Movement.

Hall Laurie Calhoun suffered a heart attack on Wednesday morning, September 4, 1935, following one of his famous radio sermons at the Nashville Central Church of Christ. He experienced another attack later that same day and died at nine o'clock in the evening. He was seventy-two years old. Would that he could have lived to preach the gospel of Christ for at least a decade more! He was buried in Woodlawn Memorial Park following the funeral services at the War

Memorial Building, the only place in Nashville large enough to accommodate the number of people who desired to attend. When his wife died on October 30, 1953, at the age of eighty-three, she was buried beside the remains of her beloved husband. The physical remains of Hall Laurie and Mary Etta Calhoun lie side by side in the Woodlawn Memorial Cemetery, waiting for the voice of God to bid them come forth from the grave to the resurrection.

So, here and now, the voice of Hall Laurie Calhoun is quiet which echoed across the city of Nashville and into remote towns and countrysides. The exceptional mind is at rest after warring against conflicts without and within—and is winning at last. The efforts which he put forth in behalf of the kingdom yet speak. He did what he could, and so he waits, surely with confidence, along with other soldiers of the cross and those giant contenders of the plea of the Restoration Movement and the pattern of New Testament Christianity.